Evolution and Creationism
in the Public Schools

Evolution and Creationism in the Public Schools

A Handbook for Educators, Parents and Community Leaders

ANGUS M. GUNN

McFarland & Company, Inc., Publishers
Jefferson, North Carolina, and London

The Scripture quotations contained herein are from the *New
Revised Standard Version Bible,* copyright © 1989 by the
Division of Christian Education of the National Council of the
Churches of Christ in the U.S.A., and are used by permission.
All rights reserved.

All illustrations are by Paul Giesbrecht

LIBRARY OF CONGRESS CATALOGUING-IN-PUBLICATION DATA

Gunn, Angus M.(Angus Macleod), 1920–
    Evolution and creationism in the public schools : a
handbook for educators, parents and community leaders /
Angus M. Gunn.
        p.   cm.
    Includes bibliographical references and index.

    ISBN 0-7864-2002-2 (softcover : 50# alkaline paper)

    1. Creationism—Study and teaching—United States.
    2. Evolution (Biology)—Study and teaching—United States.
    3. Religion in the public schools—United States.   I. Title.
    BS652.G86   2004
    379.2'8—dc22   2004018788

British Library cataloguing data are available

Cover photographs © 2004 PhotoSpin

Manufactured in the United States of America

McFarland & Company, Inc., Publishers
  Box 611, Jefferson, North Carolina 28640
   www.mcfarlandpub.com

To the Newtons, Pasteurs, and Curies of tomorrow

To the Newtons, Pasteurs, and Curies of tomorrow

Acknowledgments

I am indebted to many people for the ideas expressed in this book: the members of my family, colleagues from the University of British Columbia, the staff of the National Center for Science Education, and people from other associations of science educators. I am grateful for Sir John Polkinghorne's writings and for his personal observations on creationists' rejection of factual data. I thank the many state experts in science education from all across the United States who shared the triumphs and frustrations they experienced in their quest for excellence. National leaders in the fields of science and philosophy, too numerous to name, assisted me through their publications. Lastly, and certainly not least, a special thank you goes to Lisa Gunn who unearthed several valuable references for me.

Contents

List of Figures and Charts

Introduction

The conflict between biological evolution and creationism has been part of U.S. public school education for almost all of the twentieth century and today it shows little signs of abating. It stems from opposition by parents and others to the content being taught in the science classrooms of schools. The problem is unique in that it affects only the science curricula. In history, mathematics, or literature there is generally full acceptance of the content being taught. In all school subjects the content is determined by specialists who have the expertise necessary for the task. Parental rights have no place in these curricular decisions. Where did this conflict originate and why has it not been resolved? The task of this book is to trace the origins of the problem, examine the strengths that gave it longevity, and suggest ways of resolving it so that the energies of school administrators and teachers may be focused on their main task, the improvement of learning.

Over the past 100 years the conflict has been rooted in one word, "evolution," a word that has been inextricably tied to Charles Darwin, following the publication in 1859 of his book, *The Origin of Species by Means of Natural Selection; or, The Preservation of Favoured Races in the Struggle for Life*. Notice that Darwin did not use the word we have associated with his name. He avoided it for good reason, because in his day the word meant something quite different from its present day usage. Many forget that words change their meanings over time and in different contexts. The context problem is encountered when the word "theory" is used in relation to evolution. The different meanings of these two words, evolution and theory, are explained in Chapter One. For now, it is necessary to observe that all kinds of erroneous understandings of evolution keep reappearing in spoken or written form by those who interfere with the work of the schools. For some it means anti–God thinking. Others are convinced that it refers to the law of the jungle, the abrogation of all sense of right and wrong.

Darwin's theory of evolution focused for all time the many bits of scientific discoveries that had been made in previous centuries concerning the origins of life forms. Darwin worked alone for much of the time but he relied heavily on scientists from the past as well as those from his own time. It was time for him to identify the common thread in all that had been hinted at by others and Darwin came on life's stage at the right moment to do it. His theory, now accepted universally all over the world, says that all present forms of life have a common ancestry, one that goes back into billions of years of biological history. It was an idea whose time had come and its impact on society was powerful and permanent. There are more than 15 million species of life alive today and as many as 10 times that number became extinct in the past. Every single one of these life forms is or was tied to a still earlier form of life, perhaps four-billion-year-old bacteria. How is this known? There many evidences. The easiest to list is DNA, found in every inch of the body, carrying numerous genes that are similar to those of ancient bacteria.

Alongside this universal fact about the origin of life forms stands the uncertainty about the mechanisms involved in the process of forming new species. How does one species change into a different one, retaining in the process much of the DNA of its predecessor? This is a vital part of the story, and is covered in Chapter Four. Darwin, with the limited knowledge available to him in 1859, thought that the natural forces of the environment would determine which life forms would survive and which would not. He named this process natural selection. His reasons for this choice are examined in Chapter Four. In reality, Darwin's life work was focused on his basic theory. He gave limited thought to the mechanisms involved, leaving that task for others. His enemies today, the people who oppose his theory being taught in science classrooms, pick up his statements about the mechanisms involved and point out that, if he was wrong about this, maybe he was also wrong about his basic theory. The most vocal in this criticism are those who are convinced that humanity is a special creation of God, completely different from all other forms of life, and certainly not derived from the same material as bacteria or apes.

The difference between these two aspects of biological evolution is extremely important and it is necessary to keep it constantly in mind when examining the opposition to evolution. As criticisms are encountered, consider whether Darwin's ideas about natural selection or his theory of biological evolution are being critized? Certainly there is widespread rejection of all aspects of Darwin's work. Creationists make broad, non-scientific claims that their views on the history of life are just as valuable as the theory of evolution. These people have little acquaintance with biology and readily admit it, but they insist that what they have to say ought to be included in science courses. Their claims are further compounded by the many viewpoints represented by the word creationist. Perhaps, if only they had a better understanding of Darwin's theory, they would not keep pressing for the inclusion of their ideas in the science classroom. Change might be possible because almost all of their arguments before school boards and legislatures actually deal with the origin of life on earth, a subject that has nothing to do with Darwin's theory of biological evolution.

Lawrence Lerner, who examined levels of achievement in biological science all across the country and published his findings, concluded that more than a third of all U.S. states fail to do an acceptable job. His work will be examined in more detail in Chapter Six. Why are so many states failing? Surely they know that the impact of science on personal lives and the national destiny is now so great that young people need to know all they can about this important subject. How can they understand DNA, the dramatic implications of the Genome Project and its implications for curing diseases, or the more recent findings from brain research unless they are given a good foundation in scientific thinking while at school? The sad fact is that a majority of Americans, because of misguided views about biological science, would prefer to prevent the teaching of good science. Gallup, in 2000, found that 68 percent

3

of all Americans hold an anti-science view. The Gallup organization earlier discovered that a very large number of science teachers hold these same anti-science views. With this level of opposition to good science it is no surprise that the subject easily becomes a political issue rather than an academic one. As can be seen, this is exactly what has been happening and continues to happen at all levels of the school system.

There was a long period of confused thinking following the publication of Darwin's book. By the early 1920s for example, feelings on the subject ran so high that state after state introduced laws forbidding the teaching of any kind of evolution in public schools. In the course of the decade 1920 to 1930, no less than 37 bills were introduced into state legislatures to make the teaching of evolution illegal. Not all of these were passed into law but they represented the kind of thinking that occurred at that time. Half of the biology texts that were published made no reference whatever to evolution. This period of time will be examined again in Chapter Three, and the influences that lay behind the decisions that were made will be considered. The most celebrated outcome in the case of John Scopes will also be shown. The attitude prevalent in those years persisted into the 1950s with one of the most widely circulated texts on biology for schools avoiding the use of the word "evolution" in all of its 600 pages. Darwin's theory was described as "The hypothesis of racial development." In all of that 30-year period of time there were large numbers of citizens convinced that evolutionary thinking was evil, liable to destroy public morality.

Occasionally in recent times there were events that seemed more like the 1920s than the 1990s. Kansas in 1999 elected a board of education that decided to make it illegal to include any references to evolution and any references to an ancient earth in the science curriculum for schools. The decision was reversed a year later but it is still remembered as one of the major battles between evolutionists and creationists and it triggered a new wave of opposition to good science. It also confirmed that the issue is more political than academic. During the presidential campaign of 1999, shortly after the Kansas decision was made, Vice President Gore eagerly supported the Kansas decision. Later, when he knew it was contrary to decisions of the U.S. Supreme Court, he changed his mind and said that it should be taught in some other part of the curriculum. George Bush also defended the Kansas decision during the same campaign. Do these leaders not understand that they of all people must defend good science? Whether it is robotics (so brilliantly demonstrated in the two successful launches to Mars early in 2004) or nanotechnology (working with extremely small things), all are deeply involved in the outcomes of every new scientific break-through. Every high school student, not just those specializing in science, needs to learn a certain amount of science.

Throughout the last quarter of the twentieth century, many legal challenges were launched by creationists claiming that bio-logical evolution was not the only valid method of teaching the his-tory of life. Some of these challenges were settled at lower courts, and some went all the way to the U. S. Supreme Court. In every case, decisions were settled in favor of evolution as the proper and only method for teaching the history of life. The following is typ-ical of the various decisions that were handed down: creation sci-ence does not qualify as a scientific theory. Scientific explanations focus on what can be examined experimentally, not on the origin of life. The theory of biological evolution assumes the existence of life and studies how it evolved after it originated. It does not pre-suppose either the absence or the presence of a creator. Why then, in flagrant opposition to the law of the land, do so many insist on including creationism in the teaching of science? Do they not understand the nature of scientific data? To some extent they do, but a lack of understanding of some aspects causes concern. The fact that humans and apes have the same genes gave rise to the idea that humans are descended from apes. That is like saying a woman descended from her sister because they have the same genes.

The central reality in the conflict between biological evolution and creationism is that they represent two domains of knowledge and they should never have been treated as two aspects of one sub-ject. One field of knowledge, represented by science, deals with real world data that can be examined experimentally by many different scientists. The other, represented by creationism, deals with mat-ters of faith and relates for the most part to the origins of life as told in the Bible. Stephen Jay Gould in *Rocks of Ages*, takes an example from the life of Jesus to illustrate the fundamental difference between these two domains. He selected the following passage from the Bible for this purpose. It is taken from John's Gospel, chapter 20, verses 24 to 29:

> Thomas, one of the twelve, was not with them when Jesus came. So the other disciples told him, we have seen the Lord. But he said to them, unless I see the mark of the nails in his hands and put my finger in the mark of the nails and my hand in his side, I will not believe. A week later his disciples were again in the house and Thomas was with them. Although the doors were shut, Jesus came and stood among them and said peace be with you. Then he said to Thomas, put your finger here and see my hands. Reach out your hand and put it in my side. Do not doubt but believe. Thomas answered him, my Lord and my God. Jesus said to him, have you believed because you have seen me? Blessed are those who have not seen and yet have come to believe.

Thomas gained the epithet doubting because of this passage. Gould points out that Jesus took note of what happened and commented on its effect on Thomas but then added the critical comment, according to Gould, of pronouncing a blessing on those who would arrive at certainty indirectly by faith. Jesus knew that this would be the normal mode of knowing for all his followers. Near the end of the New Testament canon, a reflective writer traces the history of this particular way of knowing. His statement is found in Hebrews chapter 11. Verse two from this chapter relates to the fundamental nature of creationist understanding: By faith we understand that the worlds were prepared by the word of God so that what is seen was made from things that are not visible. This way of knowing is as valuable and as reliable as scientific knowledge. Those who believe in the validity of historic Christianity have knowledge that is based on faith. Scientists who think that scientific understandings are better than those of faith when it comes to Christinity are being inconsiderate neighbors. Similarly, Christians who think that matters of faith are more important for the well-being of individuals and society than the findings of science are being irresponsible citizens. Both domains of knowledge are valuable. One and only one belongs in science classrooms.

The conflict between creationism and evolution is far from being a purely American problem. In Turkey, a democratic Muslim nation, Harun Yahya is responsible for a science research foundation, a strong creationist network which is backed by organizations locally and internationally. Harun Yahya's books are widely circulated in Indonesia. In Australia, five percent of the population believe that the earth is thousands rather than billions of years old. South Africa, South Korea, and several countries in central Europe have a significant number of people supporting creation science, a term introduced by creationists to make their case more plausible for its inclusion in science. In Britain, the Vardy Foundation, which owns one school and approved plans for six more, teaches creationism alongside evolutionary theory. The British National Curriculum makes it clear that schools must teach Darwin's theory of biological evolution as the dominant scientific theory but it also says that students must understand how scientific controversies can result from different ways of interpreting empirical data. This recommendation refers to the second aspect of evolutionary theory, the mechanisms by which changes take place over time. This is what needs to be discussed in schools, not the origin of life.

A cursory reading of Darwin's *Origin of Species* easily shows that evolution isn't about the origin of life. Here is what Darwin wrote at the end of his book: "There is grandeur in this view of life, having been originally breathed by the Creator into a few forms of life or into one. From so simple a beginning endless forms most beauitful and most wonderful have been, and are being evolved." Recent research confirms that life forms have their own inherent tendencies to move toward more complex forms. They do not need intrusions from outside the organic world. This is where the creationists and intelligent designers have got it all wrong. They ignore the facts of the theory of evolution. The Rev. Dr. John Polkinghorne, KBE, FRS, identifies their problem in these words: "It is sad when those who are seeking to serve the God of truth refuse to take seriously those aspects of the truth to which science can speak. It is also harmful to the Christian cause, since it gives the false impression that faith demands intellectual suicide."

Chapters Two and Five will deal with aspects of the evolution-creationism problem never before covered in other books on the same subject. Chapter Two traces the long history of conflicts between scientists and the established church, conflicts that are often mistakenly assumed to no longer be present. Chapter Five is a detailed study of the early chapters of Genesis in the light of scientific evidence. This part of the Bible is quoted by almost all creationists to support their theory of creation science. Underneath all that may be said and done to secure higher standards in the teaching of science in schools lies the reality of widespread public and therefore political support for adding non-scientific content. At times many are inclined to wonder if the conflict is entirely a political issue rather than an academic one. Every year new proposals like the following are presented in state legislatures: Late in 2003, against the wishes of both department of education officials and the state organization of science teachers, a large number of legislators presented two bills to the Michigan House of Representatives. One of them included the following statement: "In the science standards for middle and high school, all references to evolution and natural selection shall be modified to indicate that these are unproven theories by adding the phrase, describe how life may be the result of the purposeful, intelligent design of a Creator." The final chapter of this book documents a few of the excellent programs in biological science being followed in some states.

ONE

Defining Terms

The *Concise Oxford Dictionary* says that creationism is "the belief that the universe and living organisms originated from specific acts of divine creation." The same dictionary says that evolution is "the process by which different kinds of living organisms are believed to have developed from earlier forms, especially by natural selection." These two definitions provide a useful beginning to this chapter for two reasons: (1) to underline the necessity of using reputable sources for the meanings of the words we use, and (2) to distinguish the dictionary meanings of words from the technical usages of the same words by scientists. Why do I say this? Because there are numerous occasions in the biological evolution–creationism debate where these two guidelines are ignored.

Theory

Take as an example the scientific usage of the word "theory." It means rigorously established and strongly supported ideas about, and descriptions of, real world data that were obtained through observation, experimentation, and analysis. This usage is always open to question as new discoveries are made but, at any given time, it is only employed when years of research by many scientists have confirmed the truth of an explanation for a particular set of events in the natural world. There is no guesswork about it as the most common dictionary definition would suggest. Rather it is a fact and the longer it is supported by additional research, the firmer the theory becomes. For this reason the theory of evolution is one of the best established facts about the biological world. One hundred and fifty years of experimental work have repeatedly confirmed its truth.

Recently, a director of science education in New Mexico was so frustrated by repeated difficulties with the phrase "theory of evolution" that he changed the normal wording of the curriculum guide. In his own mind there was no uncertainty about the accuracy of the theory of evolution but in the minds of everyone else in his community the use of the word "theory" meant uncertainty. Try as he would he could not change that mentality. People insisted that a theory is simply an idea, with a large degree of uncertainty. Their dictionaries told them so. They were unwilling to accept the difference between everyday and scientific usage. The end result was that all the curriculum guides for schools had to be changed so that the word "evolution" replaced the former phrase "theory of evolution." Was this the triumph of ignorance or was it an example of failure on the part of scientists to explain their work and its associated terminology?

Evolution

It is a similar story regarding the word "evolution." While it proved to be acceptable in the particular case of New Mexico, it is far from recognition elsewhere. Language gets in the way of an understanding again and again. The theory of evolution is a perfectly clear factual statement about the common origin of all life forms, acknowledged throughout the world. However, the word "evolution" appears in contexts other than in the phrase "theory of evolution" and in many of these cases there is no suggestion that we are dealing with scientific data. We talk about the evolution of cameras, trucks, language, clocks, and computers. We also talk about the evolution of human societies, river systems, and air travel. We need to remember that the word evolution is used in these different ways. Creationists in particular need to understand that there are different uses of the word.

Scientific Method

Scientific method is easily explained with a look at what happens in schools as science is being taught. Any science subject will do for this purpose: physics, chemistry, biology, or earth science. It's a subject that is easy to recognize in any school. Beakers, bottles of chemicals, scales, and measuring instruments of all kinds lie around. Everything is a hands-on experience, with lots of measuring and comparing. The essence of the subject is a method, not a body of knowledge. That is why any branch of science will do. It's a way of learning rather than what is learned, but that does not minimize the importance of what is learned. Few parents and community leaders recognize the difference between content and method in the learning and teaching enterprise.

Scientific method is not some new thing. For most of the twentieth century and still continuing at the present time, the dominant influence in the schools of America was good scientific method. It may come as a surprise to the many who advocate creationism that there are very few living Americans who are unfamiliar with this heritage from their school years. The exceptions might be those who attended inadequate schools or were living in other countries during their school years. The educational leader who introduced and sustained this method of teaching science was John Dewey and his method can be seen in most schools at the present time in the day-to-day activities of teachers and students. It has nothing to do with the philosophy of science or the epistemology of knowledge or the origin of life on earth, all of which are important subjects for study in other settings. John Dewey used the five senses—tasting, seeing, touching, feeling and hearing—in different locations to develop and test ideas arising from local experiences. The differences between subjects lay in the content selected but the method was always the same.

John Dewey dominated the educational system of North America for most of the first half of the 20th Century and his method of teaching science persisted for the rest of the century. It continues today. Dewey is an extraordinary name in the history of education. His ideas were early and revolutionary and they caught the imagination of scholars all over the world. Perhaps no other educator within the past 400 years received comparable acclaim. His books and his lectures were welcomed all over the world. Some educators used Dewey's method of teaching science before Dewey's time, but Dewey revolutionized these earlier practices by selecting content that was so popular with both parents and students that the subject of science blossomed into a position of high status throughout the 1920s. That is to say, Dewey's methods were universally accepted, but battles over biological evolutionary content remained. All of that good history of exemplary methods in science changed in 1957 when the Soviet Union launched its famous Sputnik rocket and America awoke to the threat that the communists might be ahead of it in science achievements.

New Curricula in Science

The public response at the time of Sputnik could be described as near panic. There was widespread alarm about what came to be known as the education gap, the feeling that an ominous disparity existed between the quality of American science education and its counterpart in the Soviet Union. Large grants of money were provided by the National Science Foundation (NSF) to create specialized curriculum projects in science in order to raise levels of achievement. At first the NSF funded projects in the hard sciences (physics and chemistry), then extended them to other sciences, and still later—all within a decade of Sputnik's launch—to social sciences. The phrase "social science" alarmed members of Congress. It seemed to them to be the same as communism. Wisely, educators invented the term "behavioral science" in order to avoid unnecessary conflict. All went well until three successful projects, Biological Sciences Curriculum Study (BSCS), Earth Science Curriculum Project (ESCP), and Man: A Course of Study (MACOS) appeared.

In BSCS, as one would expect, scientists and educators accepted the theory of biological evolution as an established fact and developed a large part of the project's content and methodology around it. Activities were designed for students to demonstrate how organisms adapt to their physical environment and how common characteristics like DNA in different forms of life illustrate their common origin. In ESCP, the fact that the earth's age stretched back for more than four billion years was a central theme, and various studies of rocks, climate, and earthquakes were employed to show how things change over long periods of time. MACOS was centered in the discipline of anthropology and so examples of less developed societies were selected for the project, including the Inuit of Northern Canada and the Bushmen of the Kalahari Desert in Southern Africa. In both of these societies the need to secure food for survival was highlighted. Appropriate activities were designed for students to show how humans were able to live in these two very different environments.

All three projects happened to coincide in time with revolutionary discoveries in science. The findings about DNA were only 10 years old when teaching materials from BSCS began to appear in schools. The general public, already quite suspicious of scientific findings as will be shown more clearly in Chapter Three, was shocked by suggestions that humans and animals share many of the same genes. They thought that humans must be completely different from animals. New research also proved that continents moved into single land masses about every 250 million years, and this finding had just been published as ESCP reached its final stage of production. Again, the general public was faced with new and irrefutable evidence about the earth's history. Implicit in the discovery of the earth's movements lay proof of its age, over four billion years old.

As these new curriculum projects reached schools across the country, public ire began to rise. The strongest criticisms were addressed to MACOS, perhaps because the data was so obviously at variance with life's values as we see them today. Part of this project was developed through a cooperative agreement between Harvard University and the National Film Board of Canada (NFB), and the content was displayed on film rather than print material. One NFB film described life in an Inuit village above the Arctic Circle. Among the practices mentioned in the film was the custom of a man borrowing someone else's wife in order to keep warm on a long journey across the ice if his own wife was not well enough to accompany him. Another activity was the abandoning of grandparents, taking them for a walk on the ice and leaving them there. This was done when they became too old to keep up with the rest of the family during seasonal migrations. Protest rallies against MACOS took place in many locations across the country, complaints were made at public meetings in schools, and numerous negative editorials appeared in newspapers. It was claimed that the moral character of America's youth was being undermined, the same complaint that used to feature whenever evolution was included in the curriculum.

One outcome of the new approach to science was a rejection of John Dewey and all of his ideas. He was seen as the one who had introduced and sustained poor science, now seen as the cause of national decline and a threat to national survival. Progressive education, the style of teaching that was almost synonymous with John Dewey's name, was blacklisted. Demands appeared for a return to specific content in the sciences, reminiscent of former days when the role of the teacher was seen as compelling students to learn and memorize content whether they understood it or not. So misguided was public reaction to the education gap that parents, supported by their political leaders, demanded a return to old-fashioned, nineteenth-century ways of learning. The form of teaching that emerged is still present all across America. It requires students to memorize and understand as best they can fixed bodies of content, their competence being frequently tested by exams. This style of teaching science was and is, unfortunately, strongly supported by creationists because it shifted the work of the classroom away from investigating evolution.

One of the sad aspects of the neglect of good methods of teaching science came from subsequent reports on the work of the NSF projects. Dewey's method of teaching science had been consistently employed in these reform projects, using the latest versions of subject matter content. It was his use of old subject matter that led to the rejection of Dewey and his progressive education in the post–Sputnik years. In their obsession with catching up with the Soviets, politicians and the public had thrown out, as it were, the baby with the bath water. As a result, many of the designs for improving the teaching of science were never acknowledged by educational leaders. Illustrations from two of the NSF projects show how Dewey's methods were employed. The Biological Sciences

Study at one time wanted to show quite young children how organisms adapt to their environment. This is one of the great themes of evolution, but for the young it has to be demonstrated in simple illustrations they can understand. The word evolution is far too abstract a word to use with them.

A worm was placed on a sloping board with an incentive that only a worm could understand located at the top of the board. As the worm began to crawl upward the children are instructed to steepen the board's angle of slope and observe the worm's reaction. They noted that it immediately altered its angle of ascent but still continued to climb toward the bait at the top. This behavior, at the level of understanding of a young child, is an example of the great principle of adaptation to one's physical environment. Why creationists would object to this method of teaching evolution remains a mystery. It is also a rather strange reaction on their part because Dewey's methods of teaching science are similar to those employed by Jesus as recorded in the first four books of the New Testament.

A second example is taken from Man: A Course of Study. In this case, a more sophisticated example of adjustment to environment is played out in the lives of the Kalahari Bushmen of Southern Africa who have to survive amid very inhospitable surroundings. By investigating the items scattered around a typical camp fire, senior students discover the creative ways employed by the Bushmen as they live out their daily lives. These Kalahari Bushmen became famous as a result of the film *The Gods Must be Crazy*, in which the normally simple bushman life is disrupted by a coke bottle falling from a passing plane. The added value of the film is seen in its portrayal of the role of culture in interfering with our reactions to unexpected environmental developments.

Fortunately, the remarkable findings of the Genome Project of the 1990s and recent developments in brain research restored the validity of Dewey's method and convinced many educational leaders that it was a big mistake to abandon his method when they discarded progressive education. It is now only a matter of time before Dewey's long-standing method of teaching science is once again accepted by political and educational authorities. Teachers will then be free to teach science in the way they already knew to be best.

Dewey's Teaching Method

What then, is this good method for teaching science? It is a five-stage sequence of investigations and it is a practice followed today by research scientists as much as by young people in the school system. The first stage is simply experience. In Dewey's mind, experience was the starting point in all scientific thinking. It could be part of field studies when young people are taken on an investigative trip to a garden, a forest, or a science museum. To Dewey, thinking must never be separated from either the skills or the content related to a learning activity. Thus the empirical situation, the place of experience, whether at home or inside or outside the classroom, is always the starting point in scientific thinking. The second stage is the problem. By this is meant the unexpected detail that one encounters in the course of experience. It may be a puzzle, something interesting, or an item related to things already familiar in another setting. A young child while playing with building blocks may discover that they cannot be fitted together as shown on the cover of the box containing them. A research scientist experimenting in a lab can similarly encounter an unexpected outcome.

One of the best illustrations of these first two steps is found in Darwin's account of his own research which is included in Chapter Three. Furthermore, it has often been said that some of the greatest discoveries were made in science when the scientist was busy working on an unrelated experiment, so a problem or an interest can appear in any situation. A genuine problem must develop within the experiential situation in order to stimulate thinking. It cannot be something imposed from the outside, even by a teacher, although the teacher can contrive experiences so that there is a likelihood of problems arising. But, whatever the source, the problem is the critical part of stage two. The student personally experiences something that raises questions, that seems to be a difficulty, or is not obvious, and so there is an uncertainty that sets the stage for further investigations. It is important that this problem be a very personal one, something that the student wants to pursue.

The third stage is called the data, collecting information that might help solve the problem. Young people, when they have something on their mind, will talk about it with other students, will explore around, try to find out relevant information elsewhere. They will talk to the teacher, with whom hopefully there is a good working relationship, and they may read about it. The source of their information is not important. Only its usefulness to their quest matters. The fourth stage is the generation of hypotheses, or ideas about possible solutions. Having accumulated a lot of facts, the student can suggest possible explanations. This is not a resolution of the problem, but only a procedure for planning how to test each of the suggested explanations. The fifth stage is testing. Each idea is tested in turn within new similar situations to see if it fits there. If it fails it is discarded and another one is tried out. Through such successive tests some ideas are discarded while others are tried out further.

It is very important at this point to realize that in science, one doesn't go around proving something as being right or wrong. Rather it is a process of disproving things that don't fit. Scientific inquiry therefore proceeds by a series of stages of rejecting hypotheses that don't fit and retaining those that do. It would be of great help for the discussion of biological evolution and creationism if creationists also worked in this way, using established measures to determine what fits. Dewey's five-stage method for science—experience, problem, data, hypothesis, and testing—was not absolutely new. Scientists had used it many times before him. Dewey's contribution was to put his method in contexts that made it popular for both parents and students.

It sometimes helps when considering questions of broad application if one looks at a question from the point of view of another country outside of North America. During the decade that followed World War II, a large number of U.S. educational experts went to Japan to assist in reforming its educational system. The teaching of science received special attention. One group of United States experts decided to introduce a curriculum in science and try it out experimentally in a number of school districts. Within a year, schools throughout the entire country began to take notice of this experiment.

It turned out that Dewey's methods were already well known in the country but for some reason had previously been neglected except in a few "Dewey" private schools. Within a period of another five years, however, the entire country had adopted the Dewey method of teaching science and results began to show up not only in the performance of students in the universities of Japan, but in their competitions with other countries around the world. Twenty-five years after the educational experts from the United States had left the country, Japan competed in an international science competition which involved 19 other countries. Japan's 10-year-olds ended up first amongst the competitors and the 14-year-olds came second. It was a resounding success for the Dewey method of teaching science.

The difficult question that arises, though perhaps not central to the subject of biological evolution and creationism but nevertheless important, is why the standards of achievements in science in the United States are not as high as other countries that use the same Dewey method of science teaching. Is it because there is enormous interference with science teaching by pressure from creationists all across the country? The fact that so many citizens of the United States insist on having creationist ideas included in the science curriculum may explain why schools are not always free to follow the Dewey method of teaching science. The important point to note as the description of the Dewey method is covered is that the work of the schools is no more and no less than the investigation of what can be observed. Those aspects of science that do not involve direct observation have no place in the teaching of science in schools.

Creationists

While there is a common link in their different interpretations of the Bible, creationists are far from being a unified group like scientists when it comes to their approach to the teaching of science. Their different viewpoints should therefore first be identified. A large number of them take the first few chapters of the Bible to be real history and they read it as one would read and interpret a book on the history of the United States. They conclude that creation occurred in six 24-hour days, that Adam and Eve were the first man and woman on earth, and that death was introduced into a perfect original creation because of the disobedience of Adam and Eve. They see Noah's flood as a world-wide event which destroyed most forms of life and greatly affected the processes operating on the surface of the earth. They believe that the Bible and true science are in full harmony with each other. Within this group, which many call *literalists*, there is a smaller number who subscribe to the ancient Hebrews' understanding of the cosmos.

This ancient image of the universe is illustrated in Chapter Five, Figure 5.1, and those who see it as a true description of the universe are known as **flat earthers**. Figure 5.1 features a solid dome standing above a flat earth. Above this dome is a quantity of water, the source of rain, and beneath the earth lies another vast source of water. **Geocentrists**, a second group of creationists, accept that the earth is spherical but deny that the sun is the center of the solar system. Their view of the cosmos is essentially the same as that of the flat earthers. A third group, **young-earth creationists**, are convinced that the earth is less than 10,000 years old. They reject the findings of physics, chemistry, and geology. Their chief spokesperson, Henry Morris, is the founder of the Institute for Creation Research. He is probably the most influential creationist of the late twentieth century.

Group four consists of **old-earth creationists**. These people accept the established positions of scientists regarding the age of the earth but they insist that God has been personally involved as an active causal agent in the observed changes. The **gap creationists**, the fifth group, build a whole philosophy around a perceived difference between *Genesis 1:1* and *Genesis 1:2*. They see a huge temporal gap between these two verses based on the assumption that *Genesis 1:1* describes an ancient pre–Adamic creation which was destroyed. Then, in *Genesis 1:2*, God restores the creation in six days. Thus, overall, verses 1 and 2 provide an account of an ancient earth and a quick restitutive creative work. **Day-age creationists**, the sixth type, accommodate scientific findings by treating the six days as long periods of time, each possibly as long as millions of years. They claim that the sequence of creation can be compared to the fossil record in that plants come before animals and humans appear last.

Progressive creationism, the seventh in this series, accept the findings of modern physical science in terms of such data as the Big Bang, but rejects some aspects of biological science. For instance, descent with modification is rejected in favor of God having intervened to create certain large groups of organisms. Thus, in their view, earlier forms of life are not genetically related to later ones. **Intelligent design creationists**, the eighth, are a modern equivalent of natural theology, a view that dates back to the writings of Paul in the New Testament and reinforced from time to time by others. The classic illustration used by these creationists is that of a person finding a watch and concluding that it could never have come into existence by chance. Similarly, they say the apparent signs of order, purpose, and design in life today constitute evidence of a creator.

Evolutionary creationists and **theistic evolutionists** can be grouped together as the ninth type because they are almost identical. In these perspectives God is seen as using evolution to change life and everything else in the universe according to his plan. There is some uncertainty about how much God intervenes in his creation and amid this uncertainty theological questions rather than scientific ones dominate. For example, the Roman Catholic Church (RC) fully accepts the common definition of biological evolution, namely that all life came from ancient simpler forms. However, in the RC view, God had to intervene to create the human soul in humans. The Pope confirmed this position in 1996 but forgot to mention that animals also have souls. Variants of this view, that humans are unique in the history of life, are common to all creationists.

The tenth and last version is made up of the **materialist evolutionists**, who follow a philosophical critique of evolution popularized by Phillip Johnson. In his writings, Johnson argues that because all science is concerned with the material world it is therefore philosophically materialistic. In other words, the supernatural does not exist for scientists. This is clearly not the case. There are many outstanding scientists who are also Christians.

All of the ten kinds of creationists have some common characteristics. Knowing their differences is helpful when explaining why evolution and creationism are in conflict. It is important to add here that, whatever may be the relationship of creationism to science in schools, the beliefs of creationists must be respected as fully as those of evolutionists. Many of the world's top scientists hold a strong set of Christian beliefs and are convinced that their faith in Christ holds a destiny of unbelievable value both now in this life and hereafter.

These scientists, like many others, find in the book of Genesis strong support for their faith. They see the writers of these chapters as having genuine transcendent experiences of their creator, experiences that are relevant to their own lives. However, the words employed to record these experiences carry all the limitations of language and culture in the minds of the narrators. The Bible was not dictated in contemporary English from a voice above. The timeless and the infinite have to be expressed in ways that others can understand what was intended. Therein lie all the possibilities for misunderstandings. There is no evidence that the transcendent experiences recorded in Genesis included data on either the form or the time in which the universe and its contents took shape. Thus it is with interpretations of the accounts that problems arise. This aspect of the Bible will be discussed in Chapter Five.

Scientist Claims

Only by proper usage of words and norms of language usage can there be any clarity in discussions and debates. One mistake that scientists sometimes make is going beyond their data, making statements about the origin of life for example. There isn't really a basis for this, as the topic lies outside the field of mainstream science. A scientist may speak about it as a citizen but the fact that he or she is a scientist conveys the impression that the statement is based on scientific findings. Scientists often do a poor job of informing the public about their specialist fields of knowledge. A better performance in this area would be of help to the field. It's a weakness that may have stemmed from the early days of science at the beginning of the twentieth century when there was a degree of arrogance about the potential of this new field. Extravagant claims for its power were often voiced.

There was also a notion of objectivity in those days. Scientists felt they could avoid bias by sticking closely to the evidence at their disposal so the end result of their work would be factual, untouched by personal opinion. Michael Polanyi exploded this myth. In his book *Personal Knowledge*, he showed how all humans are influenced by what he called tacit knowledge. This is defined as an unconscious awareness of data derived from past experience and one's prevailing culture. A person may think that a particular action is based on facts completely outside himself or herself. Polanyi has shown that such is never the case. Tacit knowledge affects every thought and every action. Only by large numbers of separate but similar activities by many scientists in different locations can one be sure that personal bias is eliminated.

Charles Darwin, in his introduction to *The Origin of Species*, says "no doubt errors will have crept in though I hope I have always been cautious in trusting to good authorities alone." The full context for this quote will be found in Chapter Three. Great scientists have always been aware of their own human weaknesses, long before the time of Michael Polanyi. So, when Darwin says that the development of all forms of contemporary life came from simple forms four billion years ago, the statement is backed by thousands of experiments by thousands of scientists over a long period of time. It is a very different story with creationists. They do not base their reasoning on experimental fact. Their styles of reasoning and their claims for scientific relevance is what will be considered next.

Creationist Claims

Creationists often argue against the authenticity of the basic theory of evolution and the age of the earth. The positions taken by creationists on both of these major themes are covered in this section.

One common approach among creationists is to point out individual details in the fossil record for which scientists have no answer. It's an approach frequently used by politicians to weaken the position of an opponent in order to gain a hearing for alternative views. The implication with reference to Darwin's theory is that it must be wrong because there are things in the history of life for which his theory provides no answer. For people who are not well acquainted with Darwin's theory this type of reasoning is often accepted as valid. They accept it, not because they are stupid and fail to see its illogical character, but because they already have a negative attitude toward evolutionary theory and are willing to grasp at any straws that support an anti–Darwinian position. They conveniently forget that scientists are always confronted with unresolved problems. It is the very nature of their work.

Typical of the one-liners presented by creationists in order to gain a hearing is the problem of the bombardier beetle, an insect with an extraordinary mode of self preservation. It forcefully ejects a hot liquid when attacked. To date, among the millions of fossils discovered, there are none that seem to be precursors of this beetle. Scientists know quite well that gaps of this kind are common in the fossil sequences. Water and wind erosion, landslides, or lava eruptions can permanently destroy organic matter. Occasionally there is a rich and varied deposit of fossils that make up for losses in other places. The 500-million-year-old Burgess Shale of eastern Canada is one of these rare deposits and evolutionary paleobiologists have been investigating it ever since it was first discovered. It makes no sense whatever to criticize, as creationists do, the gaps in scientific knowledge that are well known to scientists, or to use these gaps as evidence in support of totally unrelated ideas.

The limited range of knowledge in Darwin's time is rarely understood today except by people who know about mid-nineteenth-century life in England. Darwin's circumstances, interests, and limited information led him to emphasize natural selection, which is essentially a random process, as the explanation for changes. He added that there might be other explanations but his choice was natural selection as the most likely one. The reason for this is that Darwin paid little attention to the mechanisms determining changes in groups of organisms. His focus was almost totally concentrated on the basic theory, that all contemporary forms of life, and the many millions now extinct, were derived from simpler earlier forms of life. If Darwin were alive today, enjoying all the benefits of DNA discoveries and brain research, he would be the first to enter the debate about mechanisms and discount the idea that there is only one causal factor. This question will be discussed in detail in Chapter Four.

As an illustration of the limitations under which Darwin worked consider the word, "evolution," which happens to be one that he never used. It's a word that has not always carried its present day meaning. In England of the 1850s, evolution meant the unfolding of something over time as part of a planned outcome. Darwin was a true scientist and refused to accept the idea that the changes he was investigating were part of a defined plan, say by some superior power such as a creator, since he had no evidence to support that. Those in his own lifetime who opposed Darwin's work were the ones who coined the word evolution. They were anxious to prove that life had a purpose. Today the same word carries a very different meaning. Because of this, as well as for many other reasons, it is important to be clear about the meanings of the words we use, especially when we use them in the context of a different place and time. It is equally important that writers be informed about the latest findings in a scientific subject before launching criticisms of that subject in a published book. For example, Robert DeHaan and John Wiester wrote some strange things in their 2001 book, *Signs of Intelligence.*

The argument DeHaan and Wiester advanced relates to data from the Burgess Shale collection of fossils and deals with both gaps and the fact that 50 of the Cambrian animals have similar body plans. In their minds all of this could not have developed randomly. Had they read Conway Morris' book *The Crucible of Creation,* they could have avoided such a simplistic account of the facts. Morris is Professor of Evolutionary Paleobiology at the University of Cambridge and a world authority on the Burgess Shale. He describes the many possible explanations for recurring body plans.

Problems of this kind keep recurring among creationists. Every instance provides an occasion for suggesting that evolution is a weak theory. Through arguments of this type an opening is created among readers or listeners for an alternative view of life history. In reality, the fossil connections between closely related species is far better than most creationists realize. Because they are not specialists, they tend to work with second-hand information.

The developing branch of biology known as cladistics deals with the ancestors of life forms, somewhat like genealogical searches in families. This will be discussed in greater detail in Chapter Four. It's relevance here is that the extinct ancestor of a particular organism may not look at all like its present-day descendant. For example, it is an error to think that humans come from apes just because they look similar. Creationists frequently consider the absence of look-alikes in the older fossils as evidence that no ancestor ever existed. Take for example the well-known fact that birds develop from reptiles. When the fossil of one particular organism known as Archaeopteryx from 150 million years ago was discovered, it proved to be a good example of something intermediate between reptiles and birds. Creationists rejected it because it lacked the features they decided it ought to possess. It still retained the teeth and bony tail of its reptilian ancestors.

The life history problem that creates the most intense interest among creationists is the one about humans. Here it is that cladistics is vital for any normal discussion. When and where did humans appear and what were their ancestors? Creationists say that humans are a created species separated by profound and unbridgeable gaps from, say, apes, even though they share overwhelming similarities in genetic and anatomical characteristics. Further, creationists will not accept the existence of modern human-type fossils 100,000 years old from Africa. Nor do they accept that humans arrived in Europe about 35,000 years ago. They tend to relegate all such findings to forms of life that are fundamentally different from humans, the species we identify as *Homo sapiens*. In contrast, there is an almost universally accepted view that modern humans as well as their nearest relatives lived in Africa more than 100,000 years ago. Anatomically they were all identical at that time. Modern humans, with their various cultural characteristics as well as the long-standing anatomical ones, date from about 35,000 years ago.

You can readily see why these dates offend many creationists. Adam and Eve cannot be the first humans on the planet. Earlier forms of life that were ancestors of, and anatomically similar to, present-day humans lived millions rather than thousands of years ago.

A summary of the evidence for the enormous stretches of time involved may be essential here.

One of the oldest methods in use is measurement of radioactive decay in selected volcanic rocks. The amount of decay gives an indication of when they were formed, that is to say when they cooled from magma and began to reveal loss of radioactivity. Creationists have picked on this measure to argue that it is not sufficiently reliable over different spans of time. This may well be true but it is only one of many measures of time and its greatest value comes when it is compared with others.

Geological research made great strides in recent times, and in so doing provided valuable information about the age of the earth. Even as far back as the early nineteenth century, geologists were convinced that certain types of rocks were older than others, although their exact ages were not known at that time. As interest in fossils developed among biologists and rocks throughout the world were searched for them, again and again the same types of fossils were discovered in rocks of the same kind. This had nothing to do with their actual ages. It only established that certain forms of life, all now extinct, lived at the same time that certain rocks were laid down. The most dramatic form of these parallels came from thousands of deep-sea cores taken from different locations in the world's oceans. These cores revealed the same sequences of rocks as had been observed on land and within them were also found microscopic fossils, each type occurring in the same kind of rock. In spite of all these coincidences, creationists pick on overthrusting in rocks, as illustrated in Figure 1.1 to argue that these interfere with rock sequences. It seems that dogmatism about the age of the earth makes people almost incapable of recognizing clear evidence to the contrary.

In the 1960s, a new geological finding ended the dispute about the earth's age. It was plate tectonics, the discovery of a series of huge rock plates on the ocean floor, some of them bigger than the total area of the U.S. These plates are always in constant, extremely slow motion. They originate at places in oceans where molten magma rises up from inside the earth through cracks in the ocean floor. As the magma is pushed away from these cracks by the force

Figure 1.1. Creationists argue that overthrusts in rock formations destroy the evidence in sequences of rock layers.

of new flows of rock from beneath, it cools and slides away on top of the underlying bedrock. These slow moving slabs of cool rock, which we call tectonic plates because of their origin, may extend downwards for many miles. Nowadays, with the aid of the global positioning system of satellites, we can measure with precision the rate at which these huge plates move. By comparing their distances from source, a precise measure of age is thus obtained. It is a computation confirmed by observing the earth's magnetic orientation in rocks at different locations. It is well known that this orientation changes from north to south and vice versa at regular intervals of less than a million years.

The positions taken by creationists on both of these major themes, authenticity of the basic theory of evolution and the age of the earth, are not strong because they do not use data and reasoning that is reliable. Their success stems from the strong support they receive from the public at large and their work is focused on securing and maintaining that support. Often the strategy employed is purely negative, pointing out some weakness, as they see it, in the data in order to gain a hearing for a very different point of view. Their thinking is if they could show errors in either of the two areas we have just been discussing, the basic theory of evolution and the age of the earth, then creationists' point of view would be a vital contribution to the school science curricula. As things stand they have nothing to contribute to schools but they represent a strong force in the political realm. Various arguments are presented by creationists in that context in the hope that public support might influence decisions at the school level. One of the most popular of these arguments relates to the supposed harmful influence of evolutionary thinking on morality.

The assumption that evolutionary theory is harmful to morality goes back as far as the late nineteenth century. It was based on two misunderstandings, that the theory attacks faith in a supreme being and that a literal interpretation of the Bible is an indispensable foundation for good living. Evolution is still a fairly new idea and it happened to coincide in time with a rejection of the historicity of the early chapters of Genesis. The impact of these developments is dealt with more fully in Chapter Three and covers the very strong reactions that followed World War I. Today's reactions bear a strong resemblance to those of the early 1920s. The Catholic Church, as was noted earlier, has insulated itself from much of the public furor by accepting the Darwinian theory of evolution fully but then adding that God implanted a soul in the *Homo sapiens* species. The Biblical account describes this as something that developed, which is closer to the theory of biological evolution. Others are tackling the issue in ways ranging from direct political action to unsubstantiated criticisms of evolutionary theory.

There is a prevailing negative attitude toward evolution. Any talk show that touches on the subject is soon overwhelmed with calls. This attitude is mainly due to ignorance, in particular ignorance about the difference between the basic theory of evolution and the mechanisms involved. Unfortunately, creationists add to the ignorance. Nancy Pearcey in *Signs of Intelligence*, asserts that the Darwin theory of evolution promotes a philosophy of naturalism which, in her words, is implacably opposed to any form of theism. Anyone who thinks like this should read Darwin's correspondence with Asa Gray, a colleague and Christian at Harvard University, with whom he first shared his theory of evolution. Here is what he wrote to Gray on one occasion, "I cannot view this wonderful universe and especially the nature of humanity, and conclude that everything is the result of brute force. I am inclined to look at everything as resulting from designed laws." Pearcey finds support from some scholars for her distortion of scientific facts and ends up with a tirade of condemnations of Darwin: no ethics, no future for humanity, no free will. With such advocates of truth, it is no surprise that confusion reigns.

The mention of design by Darwin may not be a popular idea among creationists as it is now their most widely used word. In state after state across the U.S., legislators are bombarded with bills advocating the inclusion of intelligent design in school science curricula. This represents for creationists a move away from the details of biological evolution into those of philosophy and is therefore not central to the purpose of this book. However, because it is so pervasive, with historical roots stretching back into the beginnings of Christendom, and because it is being used to change school curricula by fiat, it must be examined. As mentioned in the Introduction, in 2003 the State of Michigan had a substantial number of legislators presenting two bills advocating the inclusion of the design hypothesis as an explanation for the origin and diversity of life. All references to evolution were to be treated as unproven theories. Both Department of Education specialists and the state's Association of Science Teachers opposed the bills.

The reference to origins is a further indication of widespread ignorance. Biology teachers and specialists in evolution consistently point out that their work has nothing to do with the origin of life. Their work, they say, deals only with what already exists and judicial decisions at the U.S. Supreme Court as well as at lower levels confirm this position. To include origins would be a denial of their competence as scientists because they would have no data to examine experimentally. To complicate matters, creationists talk about the philosophy of intelligent design as a "fully-fledged scientific research program" to quote Nancy Pearcey again. It becomes increasingly difficult to exchange ideas when all the norms of language usage are abandoned in this way. How can one discuss science with Pearcey when she defines design, the modern equivalent of the age-old natural theology, as a scientific revolution equal to that of Isaac Newton?

Natural theology, the perception of design in nature, is a philosophy that goes back to Paul's writings in the New Testament. In his letter to the Romans he wrote, "Ever since the creation of the world His eternal power and divine nature, invisible though they are, have been understood and seen through the things He has made." Paul refers to humanity's inherent awareness of its creator. In the centuries that followed, writers like Augustine, Thomas Aquinas, John Calvin, and in modern times, Karl Barth and John Polkinghorne, concluded that humanity is able to see the cosmos as an ordered system because there is a congruence between it and our own natural, rational minds. Any understanding of the nature of the one who created this cosmos is based on faith, a trust in the biblical statement that an awareness of the creator was planted in every member of *Homo sapiens*. There is no other basis than faith for this so-called scientific revolution of design. Such knowledge must be respected, but it has nothing to do with scientific fact.

The creationist arguments about design do not stop at the level of biblical defense. Books have been appearing in the marketplace in recent years, defending the idea of design further, first from the presence of irreducible complexity, then on the basis of the cosmological constant, and finally as the only answer to scientific materialism. To explain, as technology enables humankind to examine inanimate and organic matter in greater and greater detail, the extraordinary complexity of virtually everything is awe inspiring. Even the tiniest part of a single cell carries a universe of detail. This, asserts the creationist, is proof of a creator's design. Maybe it is proof of human abilities. The other idea, the cosmological constant, an aspect of natural theology, relates to the orderliness of the cosmos, the existence billions of years ago of critical chemical components that one day would be essential for the formation of human life. Regarding materialism, it seems to creationists that school science is bad if it is only scientific. Are mathematics and physics also bad because they do not involve students in philosophies of design?

This chapter has been about defining terms. The reality of American life, as indicated in the Introduction, is dominated by the views of people who may not be familiar with what is defined here. Indeed most of them, as the history of the problem attests, know very little about the teaching of science in schools. This is particularly sad because, as pointed out earlier, all of them were exposed to good science teaching. Much must have been forgotten. As parents, they feel they have certain rights regarding the material being taught to their children. Thus it often happens, from time to time, in particular places, that parental groups put pressure on local schools, forcing teachers to include creationist content in their science classes even when it is against the schools' rules.

A director of science education in Arkansas actually had to cope with ignorance among teachers, not the general public. This is not an isolated case. In Arkansas, the issue of biological evolution in science classes was firmly settled by the Supreme Court of the United States years ago. Nevertheless, little has changed in parental drives to reintroduce it. In this director's words, "We are in the Bible Belt" and can only do so much. The science curriculum guide presently in operation is quite clear about the factual accuracy of the theory of evolution. In the estimate of this director, one in five teachers across the state teach it well and another fifth will make some effort to stay within the curriculum. The rest, that is to say most of the state's science teachers, will avoid teaching anything about evolution. The director is afraid that evolution will be diluted even further in the years to come. The reality, both in Arkansas and across America, is that there is always some local autonomy given to schools and nobody really knows what happens when the classroom door closes. This problem will be discussed later.

Closing Arguments

It is appropriate that the last word about definitions be given to the nation's legal authorities. Theirs is the responsibility for saying what is right and what is wrong when others cannot agree. Here are some of the decisions affecting biological evolution that were handed down by different courts over the past 40 years, beginning with an important one from Arkansas in 1968. It was the first to challenge the prevailing rejection of evolution and support of creationism that had remained in place ever since the Scopes trial of 1925. The details of that trial are in Chapter Three. The last section ended with observations about the problem of keeping creationists out of the science classrooms of Arkansas. This state was not only the first to challenge the wisdom that prevailed from 1925 onward. It is also the state that appealed twice about creationism. The second of its appeals will be described in Chapter Three because it is often identified by the name "Scopes Two."

Susan Epperson, a teacher from Arkansas, with support from many, challenged the rights of creationists to be involved in science classrooms. The case went to the U.S. Supreme Court in 1968. The Court invalidated the Arkansas statute that had prohibited the teaching of evolution. It concluded that the statute was unconstitutional on grounds that the First Amendment to the U.S. Constitution does not permit a state to require that teaching and learning must be tailored to the principles or prohibitions of any particular religious sect or doctrine.

In 1981, California's Supreme Court was asked to rule on a teacher's claim that the Board of Education's Science Framework prohibited his and his children's free exercise of religion. The Science Framework contained an anti-dogmatism clause to ensure that class discussions of origins should emphasize that scientific explanations deal with how, not ultimate causes. The Court ruled that the framework gave sufficient accommodation to the views of the teacher and it also directed the Board of Education to disseminate its decision to teachers of all science subjects, not just those dealing with issues of origin.

A case similar to the one from Arkansas in 1968 followed from Louisiana in 1987. It concerned a statute prohibited the teaching of evolution in public schools, except when it was accompanied by instruction in creation "science." The U.S. Supreme Court found that the statute was unconstitutional because it advanced the religious belief that a supernatural being created humankind. The statute, it said, impermissibly endorses religion. In addition, the Court found that the provision of a comprehensive science education program is undermined when teachers are compelled to include creation "science" with evolution.

In 1990, the Illinois Seventh Circuit Court of Appeals upheld a district court finding that the First Amendment rights of a teacher from New Lenox School District had not been violated. The teacher had been prohibited from teaching creation "science." The Court found that creation "science" was a form of religious advocacy and therefore a violation of the First Amendment's establishment clause. It further stated that religious beliefs must not be injected into the public school curriculum.

John Peloza brought action against California's Capistrano school district, its board of trustees, and various personnel at a high school in 1994, claiming that his First Amendment right to free exercise of religion was violated because he was compelled to teach evolution in biology classes. Peloza's claim that evolution is a religion was rejected and he was told not to talk with students about religion while at school, even when he was not teaching. The Court asserted that the school district had appropriately required a science teacher to teach a scientific theory in a biology class.

In 1997, the U.S. District Court that serves Eastern Louisiana rejected a policy that the Tangipahoa Parish Board of Education had put in place. The policy required teachers to read aloud a disclaimer whenever they taught evolution, pointing out to their classes that evolution is a religious viewpoint that runs counter to other religious views. The Court noted that, in the policy, the only concept from which the students were not to be dissuaded was the biblical concept of creation. While rejecting disclaimer policies the Court added that curricular proposals for intelligent design are equivalent to those for creation "science." The Parish Board twice attempted to appeal the decision but it was rejected both times.

As recently as 2000, a district court in Minnesota rejected an appeal by a high school teacher who claimed he had the right to present to his classes evidence both for and against the theory of evolution. A report from his district stated that the content of his teaching did not match the prescribed curriculum. The Court concluded that the teacher had no right to override the requirements of the curriculum, that adherence to the curriculum did not infringe his free speech rights, and that the school district was not guilty of religious discrimination.

Two

The Historical Roots
of Creationism

Creationism's roots go back a long way, about 2000 years to the beginning of Christendom. In most of that time, conflicts arising from interpretations of the Bible have been common in century after century. First it was conflict with heretics, then with scientists, and frequently the heretics were scientists. These tensions began to appear in the fourth century for a particular reason. Prior to that time, the early life of Christians had been quite different. Jesus's followers lived ordinary lives without the organizations and structures with which we are familiar today. The only religious buildings visible in a city like Rome were the temples to Jupiter, Janus, or Saturn. Christians usually met one with another in small groups in homes or caves. So informal were their activities that observers often referred to them as people with a certain way of life. Despite the simplicity of their lives, they were severely persecuted for a long period of time because they did not honor the religious practices of the Romans. Often they had to hide in the catacombs of Rome to escape capture and execution.

Their simple lifestyle would probably have been maintained indefinitely, because it was modeled on the example of Jesus, had it not been for an unexpected event in the course of the fourth century. The Roman Emperor Constantine had a vision of a cross in the course of one of his military campaigns, a vision that he claimed helped him win a major battle. As a result, he took a great interest in the Christians and early in the fourth century he issued a decree making Christianity the official religion of the empire. Immediately all the persecutions came to an end and Constantine arranged to have the entire Christian world united under one organization, the Roman Catholic Church. This new temporal power had a leader, later known as the Pope, along with many others who operated at lower levels of authority. The concept of temporal power was contrary to the views of Jesus, the founder of Christianity. He had defined his kingdom as an influence within society, not a power to govern and control people, so it is not surprising that conflicts arose as the new organization established rules regarding right and wrong forms of belief.

As long as the Roman Empire continued in power the role of the church was a religious one, administering sacramental services for the public and pronouncing blessings on the activities of the Roman authorities and military leaders. Its religious power was absolute within the empire and its status in other countries steadily rose until it became the one voice of Christianity, the official spokesperson for God in this world. Around the time of Constantine's decree a letter was discovered, purportedly from Peter, in which he had delegated his authority to the leader of the church in Rome. This authority had presumably rested with Peter on the basis of a verse in Matthew's Gospel, chapter sixteen, verse 19, in which Jesus said to Peter, "I will give you the keys of the kingdom of heaven; whatever you bind on earth will be bound in heaven, and whatever you loose on earth will be loosed in heaven." The additional validation of the letter from Peter was a valuable confirmation of the church's position as the Roman Empire disintegrated in the fifth century. It provided the one continuing link with the beginnings of Christianity and a source of authority at a time of widespread confusion. No one else was in a position to challenge it.

The church's power rested on two things, the status it had established for itself from the time of Constantine, and a literal set of interpretations of the Bible. These official interpretations became entrenched in the life of the church, and intolerance toward others increased. Those who disagreed with its teachings were severely punished. It mattered not whether disagreements came from Christians or from others. Everyone had to conform to the wishes of the church. It was difficult for individuals to disagree. The church claimed to be the only source for understanding the Bible, thus interpretations from others were quickly defined as heresy. Any person who had not been baptized by the church and participated in the benefits it offered would go to hell and be forever damned. That was the official church view. The worst fate that any person could suffer was excommunication, that is to say being removed from the benefits the church provided. It destroyed a person's prospects in life now because of the church's control within society, and it condemned the person to hell in the next life. It is difficult for people today, being so far removed in time, to understand how a country could be totally dominated by the views of one church. This is the way it was all through the Dark Age for almost a thousand years. There was little freedom of thought and science as is known today was almost nonexistent.

The memory of these conditions was stamped on the conscience of society over a very long period of time and that type of experience is not easily erased. When people today wonder how creationists still retain those ancient interpretations of the Bible, it helps to remember that long-standing traditions have great power, especially when they are backed by the fear of terrible punishment for all who try to change them. Here is an example from the thirteenth century, 900 years after the church had gained temporal power, that illustrates the extent of the church's influence at that time. King John of England, the same John who signed the Magna Carta in 1215 to limit the traditional absolute power of kings, had been instructed by the Pope to appoint Stephen Langton as Archbishop of Canterbury. King John decided to exercise his right to nominate another person. Pope Innocent the Third immediately issued a decree banning the conduct of religious services of any kind in all of England and, at the same time, excommunicating the king along with all others. This act of removing people from the benefits of the church meant that they were condemned to hell because they were outside the communion of saints. It also meant that anyone under the ban must not be offered food, shelter, or clothing. It was, for all practical purposes, a death sentence and a very powerful tool for social control. King John's response was to surrender, agree to the Pope's choice for the Archbishop of Canterbury, and hand over

England to the Pope. He received a considerable amount of money for so doing and England thus became a fiefdom of Rome.

Another glimpse of the old way of life in the 1400s is from one European university. Aberdeen University in Scotland celebrated its Quincentenary in 1995, publishing an account of its founding by the Pope 500 years earlier and outlining the continuing influence of the original charter. It was just like other universities all over Europe from that time. Everyone studied Latin, the lingua franca of the time, plus a theology which included substantial content on life in general but little on science. The location of the School of Theology was physically in the center of the campus and, in the case of Aberdeen, still is. Students could easily move from a university in one country to any other throughout Europe because the programs of study were identical. It was a theocentric age in which theology was the queen of the sciences and the Roman Catholic Church was visible at every level of society. The beliefs held by the church were completely inflexible and people had either to accept them or face the torturer until they recanted. King John's experience helps shed light on revolt against the church that occurred a little over 100 years following England's surrender to the Pope. It came from within, from one of the church's own, and hence the reaction by the church was more violent than usual. Civil wars usually are. The heretic concerned was John Wycliffe and he was determined to undermine the church's claim to be the arbiter of all Biblical interpretations.

Wycliffe and Tyndale

John Wycliffe (1330–1384) and his activities were followed up by William Tyndale (1494–1536). Both of these men were theological leaders of high rank and they reacted successively to the abuses that had developed in the church over the years. The well-known aphorism "power corrupts and absolute power corrupts absolutely" had become true in their time to a degree unmatched by all previous expressions of the Roman Catholic Church (RCC). It had been an anachronism from its beginning and after a thousand years it reached the place where all of its power was being employed to crush any opposition. John Wycliffe was born around 1330 and educated at Oxford where he earned the doctor of divinity degree in 1372. Notice that his first degree was in theology. There was no alternative if a person wanted to make progress in society. He rose quickly to the highest levels of influence in both the English church and state. Two years after graduation, King Edward III appointed him rector of Lutterworth, and later made him part of a deputation to meet at Brussels with a papal deputation to negotiate differences between the English King and the Pope.

Wycliffe's criticisms of the church found expression in a series of publications and because of his high standing these publications were circulated widely, though not as widely as he had hoped. His publications as well as his later translations of the Bible appeared before the age of printing so he was dependent on book peddlers. These were itinerant salesmen who were always ready to sell all kinds of publications, many of them not reliable. Professors at universities bought or rented manuscripts from them. They were extremely valuable agents for Wycliffe because they did not have to conform to the church's wishes and could market his banned material. Making copies of manuscripts was no small task. Reliable scribes who were not afraid to offend the religious authorities had to be hired for the task. One scribe would be able to copy four books in one period of time before his location was discovered by the church's spies and new sites had to be found. Needless to say, Wycliffe's effective criticisms of church abuses greatly upset the Pope, but two other things caused even stronger reactions.

One was Wycliffe's rejection of the church's doctrine of transubstantiation, a particularly important thing for the church because it assured unique power over its members. Anyone who offended the church's leaders could be denied access to the sacrament of transubstantiation, and therefore would be condemned to hell. This particular interpretation of the Bible was based on the ideas of Aristotle, the Greek philosopher who was a powerful influence in the RCC during its first millennium. For Aristotle, substance represented the essential nature of something while accidents described its appearance. For the church, in the eucharist, the change of the bread and wine into the body and blood of Jesus Christ in the act of consecration was the essential nature of the event. The appearance of the bread and wine did not change. If you took a photograph of them before and after the act of consecration the two pictures would be identical. The idea that the bread and wine suddenly became something else made no sense to Wycliffe. In his mind, why not call it what everyone knew it to be?

The other thing in Wycliffe's life that incensed the church was his involvement in translating the Bible into the language of the people, in this case into English. The ecclesiastical rulers had no intention of ever letting the general public gain access to the Bible in their own local language. Only the experts in the RCC could understand and interpret it. Wycliffe was able to break into this exclusive club. He led a movement for a translation of the Bible into English, and completed two translations. So effective was he in opening up access to the Bible for everyone in England that his influence continued long after his death. Lollards or Wycliffites, lay preachers, traveled around the English countryside with his writings, including copies of the Bible in the local language, not in the Latin versions used by the church. These lollards were reformers who urged people to discover the Bible for themselves. They encouraged people to exercise personal faith, criticized the church, and promoted the equality of women in all matters of faith and practice. Wycliffe died in 1428 while still in his early fifties and so escaped the torturers and the stake, a fate that would surely have overtaken him if he had lived longer. The church had already declared him a heretic over the transubstantiation doctrine. In his obituary the church further defamed him: No more dangerous heretic than Wycliffe has appeared since the birth of Jesus Christ. Nevertheless, Wycliffe insisted all his life that he had always been a loyal churchman.

As a final act of humiliation, the church decided to accord him the treatment that they wished they had provided in his lifetime, to be burned alive at the stake in order to destroy any influence he might still have on others. At least this was the hope of the church. Accordingly, 44 years after his death, by order of Pope Martin the Fifth from Rome, Wycliffe's bones were exhumed from his church in Lutterworth and taken in solemn procession under the watchful eyes of bishops and other dignitaries to a nearby hillside, the local public execution site. Bishop Fleming of Lincoln, who had authority over the church at Lutterworth, presided over the event. He first read out the 200 propositions that Wycliffe had put forward in his lifetime and that the church had condemned at a special meeting 13 years earlier. As a heretic, Wycliffe was guilty of treason against God. St. Thomas Aquinas identified it as something that separates a man from God more than any other sin. Bishop Fleming pointed out that, in the light of these things, the body of the heretic had to be taken from the consecrated ground in the church at Lutterworth and destroyed.

The dead man's remains were first dressed in the vestments that he formerly would have worn to celebrate mass so that they could be stripped from him one by one to establish his deposition from the priesthood. Bishop Fleming, at this point, accompanied by the other bishops, solemnly cursed Wycliffe and commended his soul to the devil. The double condemnation was intended to destroy him in this life and pursue his soul into an eternity in hell. Then the remains, bound in chains, were attached by the public executioner to the stake, because no member of the priesthood could be involved in the actual execution, and the fire was lit. To ensure complete destruction the skull and bones were broken into tiny fragments. Whatever remained at the end was swept into a container and thrown into the nearby river Swift.

William Tyndale was born in western England and, as a young man of 27, became chaplain to royalty following his studies at Oxford and Cambridge. He was greatly influenced by the writings and work that Wycliffe had left. He was also influenced by the work of the protestant reformer Martin Luther.

Almost from the beginning of his public career he became involved in movements that fought for church reform. At 28 he had already gained the reputation of being a heretic. His passion was to see the Bible available in the language of the people. He referred to this as wanting to see it available to the youngest boy at the plough. At the age of 30 he was busy at work on a translation of the New Testament. It was completed within a year. The work was dangerous because the Archbishop of Canterbury had decreed, some years before Tyndale was born, that the Bible should neither be translated into English nor read in English at any time and that ruling was still in force. For security and in order to take advantage of the new invention of printing, Tyndale moved to Germany. From there he was able to smuggle many copies back to England within a year. The outcry against him by the church's officials forced Tyndale into hiding, even though he was away from England. The translation of the first five books of the Old Testament was next on his agenda, and he was able to complete it five years after his New Testament.

Other translations followed until an English spy discovered him in Holland in 1535 and brought his work to a standstill. He was charged as a heretic and, like Wycliffe, he responded in clear, simple language, basing all of his defense on the Bible. His statements were clear but they were numerous and every one defined him as a heretic. "Faith alone justifies" was his typical response. Salvation flows from grace and the forgiveness of sins offered in the gospel, not from good works. He rejected the idea of purgatory and papal supremacy. He made it clear that church rulings based on human traditions cannot bind the human conscience. In addition he rejected outright the value of prayers for the departed saints, pilgrimages, and confessions to priests. He was tried as a heretic before a tribunal of three bishops in a manner similar to Wycliffe's. First he was dressed in the vestments of a priest, then disrobed. His hands were scraped with a knife to remove the oil with which he had been anointed at his consecration, and finally the bishops cursed him and committed his soul to the devil. The executioner strangled him before burning him at the stake. His last words were, "Lord open the King of England's eyes."

Copernicus, Bruno, and Galileo

Wycliffe and Tyndale concentrated their reforms on matters within the church's normal activities—differences of opinion on theological doctrines and access to the Bible by all the members of society, not just the official leaders of the church. The Bible was originally given to everyone in their own languages and Wycliffe and Tyndale wanted to restore that original pattern. In the century that followed their works the church was challenged by a very different group of reformers, scientists. Scientific thinking and research were not new. They had featured in Greek and other societies from earliest times, but for the more than 1,000 years of the church's dominance, little new science had been accomplished. The

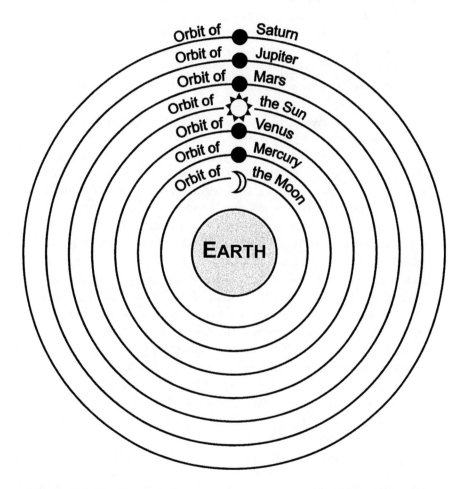

Figure 2.1. The Ptolemaic view of the cosmos was widely accepted for more than a thousand years until it was challenged by Nicholas Copernicus.

prevailing view by the time Nicholas Copernicus (1473–1543) appears is little changed from the first century AD. Figure 5.1 in Chapter 5 illustrates this early view, as well. The earth was considered to be motionless while all the stars and planets moved around it. The sun, moon, and the planets were seen to be carried around the earth in a series of complicated movements and the stars all moved together around the earth in a separate series of orbits. These views came from the Alexandrian scientist Ptolemy and the Greek philosopher Aristotle. Direct viewing of the sky was the only kind of observation possible. Telescopes had not yet been invented.

The emergence of serious scientific challenges to the church from men who were not at the centers of power was a new development and they were soon recognized as being serious and sustained. Their scholarly precision was so convincing that the church reacted violently to them, all the more because of the great intellectual gulf that lay between them. Science deals with the material world, the things around us that can be examined with our five senses and assessed by our minds. Christian leaders, unfortunately, mainly as a result of earlier philosophical ideas from Greece, had a distaste for the physical world and paid very little attention to it. Astronomy was treated as a branch of mathematics. The earth was seen as God's footstool and all of its phenomena far less worthy of study that the things of religion. Copernicus was the first to make a breakthrough from this so-called science of antiquity. His ideas were not totally new. Several before him had suggested that the earth might not be the center of the universe, but he was the first to make the concept clear, and for this he is generally regarded as the founder of modern astronomy. He was born in Poland and sent off to Cracow University in his own country to study mathematics and optics, then to Bologna in Italy for the study of canon law, without which, like Wycliffe and others before him, there would be no leadership role for him.

On his return from Italy, he was appointed a canon in the cathedral of Frauenburg where he spent a sheltered and academic life for the rest of his days. Because of his clerical position, Copernicus moved in the highest circles of power. His interests however lay elsewhere. He was always a student and his study of astronomy gradually grew to be the one that dominated his life. Investigations were carried on alone with little interference from others. He used a turret on the protective wall around the cathedral from which he could observe the skies. In 1530, he circulated his revolutionary description of the universe, *Sketch of the Hypotheses for the Heavenly*

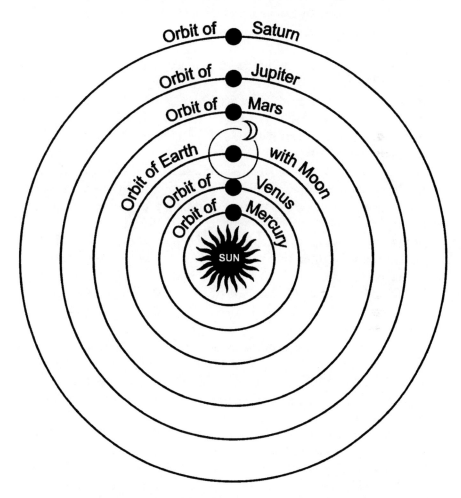

Figure 2.2. The Nicholas Copernicus view of the cosmos emerged from his direct observation of the skies without the help of a telescope.

Motions, one in which the earth is seen as rotating on its axis once daily and moving around the sun once a year. Only a few manuscript copies were made and they were given to his friends. Today, any grade six student knows all that he wrote, but in the time of Copernicus it was as startling a claim as anyone could imagine. Everyone around him was convinced that the earth was the center of the universe with the sun, moon, and planets orbiting it. The early Christian community accepted this description of Ptolemaic cosmos and it stayed as the official view right up to the time of Copernicus. The church insisted that this was a true interpretation of the Bible. Hence, anyone presenting a different cosmology would automatically be deemed a heretic. There were considerable delays in publishing Copernicus' work, largely because he insisted on numerous further investigations before he was convinced that his findings were accurate.

He was a true scientist, always questioning his own work until repeated confirmations established its reliability. So long did he wait that his discovery might have been completely lost had it not caught the attention of George Rheticus, a young German mathematics professor, who had read about him and was so interested that he paid him a visit, intending to spend a few weeks with him. Instead he stayed for two years. The first printed edition of Copernicus' completed work, *De Revolutionibus*, was finally published in 1543 when the author was on his deathbed. Like Wycliffe, he was one of the few heretics that escaped the torturers and the stake, that is to say burned alive while tied to a post in the ground. His book contained an introduction that another writer had inserted in place of Copernicus' one in order to maintain the official church position on the cosmos. As a result, Copernicus never knew that the accuracy of his work had been fully accepted by the scientific community. Nor would he know the powerful long term results of his work. It forever changed the place of humanity in the cosmos. Several years after his death another scientist, Johannes Kepler, found out who the imposter was who had inserted the false introduction. His name was Andreas Osiander, a loyal supporter of the church.

Some of the theologians who were quick to criticize the abuses of the church were slow to affirm the value of Copernicus' work.

"This fool wishes to reverse the entire science of astronomy; but sacred Scripture tells us that Joshua commanded the sun to stand still, and not the earth," was Luther's observation about Copernicus while the latter was still alive. Some years later, Luther's disciple Melanchthon observed that it is the part of a good mind to accept the truth as revealed by God and to acquiesce in it. John Calvin also repudiated Copernicus in his commentary on Psalm 93:1: "The world also is stabilized, that it cannot be moved," accompanied by the question, who will venture to place the authority of Copernicus above that of the Holy Spirit? These great reformers of the church, though they saw and opposed error in the RCC, apparently were unable to see the errors in the church's view of the cosmos. Yet Copernicus had placed clear evidence for these errors before them. What is the reason for this blindness? It is the same one that affects creationists today, a refusal to use their minds when they encounter facts that collide with entrenched convictions about the Bible.

Bruno (1547–1600) was another scientist who burst on the scene a few years after the death of Copernicus. His impact was like no other before modern times. He embraced Copernicus' work unreservedly but went far beyond it, offering theories about the cosmos that match the frontiers of present day thought. This is what he wrote in his, *Cause, Principle, and Unity.* "There is no absolute up or down, as Aristotle taught; no absolute position in space; but the position of a body is relative to that of other bodies. Everywhere there is incessant relative change in position throughout the universe, and the observer is always at the center of things." It sounds more like the famous cosmologist Stephen Hawking of Cambridge, England, than of a scientist who lived more than 400 years ago. Bruno was as close to the frontiers of cosmology as any living scientist of the present time. He probably did not have any data to match his thesis but the fact that anyone could think like that in his time is extraordinary.

It is easy to imagine the heretical reputation which Bruno created for himself in the minds of the clerical authorities. His description of an infinite, constantly—changing universe left no room for an unchanging God who was seen to be resident above the earth.

But Bruno was so naïve that he never imagined anyone would regard his ideas as heresies. He suggested that space was boundless and that the sun with its planets were but one of any number of similar systems, and further that there might be other inhabited worlds with rational beings equal or superior to us. Bruno was a prisoner in the Republic of Venice for a time, then in Rome. For six years, between 1593 and 1600 he lay in a Papal prison. None of the historical records for that time have been published or acknowledged. The only information about them comes from a visiting German scholar who was in Rome in 1600 and discovered that Bruno had been interrogated several times by the Holy Office and was then convicted of heresy by the chief theologians.

It was customary to give second chances to heretics. They could, if they wished, recant and confess their faults. Often 40 days were allowed for such soul searching. If they recanted, they would be given penances to atone for their misdeeds. Bruno was twice given opportunities to recant, but when he was interrogated afterward, he completely baffled his inquisitors with his imaginative mind. Finally, he was condemned to death by fire. Bruno's response was, "Perhaps you, my judges, pronounce this sentence against me with greater fear than I receive it." He was taken to the stake and as he was dying a crucifix was presented to him, but he pushed it away with fierce scorn. He suffered a cruel death and achieved a martyr's fame. He was not a mere religious sectarian. He was a sensitive, imaginative poet, fired with the thought of a larger vision for a larger universe. His is an incredible story that the church will never outlive.

Perhaps the best-known scientist of this period is Galileo (1564–1642). Following some false starts in first deciding to enter a monastic life and then a medical career, his parents permitted him to take up mathematics by the time he was 19 years of age. One incident from that time in his life is indicative of his scientific mind. He was attending prayers one evening at the Cathedral of Pisa and noticed the way the altar lamp swung from side to side. Using his pulse as a measure of time, since there were no watches in existence at that time, he discovered that the time of the swing had nothing to do with its width but only with the length of the pendulum.

Galileo never made use of this discovery but in later years it was used to make more accurate clocks. During the summer of 1586 he wrote his first scientific book, *The Little Balance,* a description of a technique that uses an ordinary balance as an alternative to Archimedes' method of finding the specific gravities of substances. His name will always be associated with the apocryphal story of dropping of objects from the Tower of Pisa in order to demonstrate that all of them, in opposition to Aristotle's view, would drop at the same rate, except for the influence of air.

The story says that Galileo held a feather and a stone in his hand and released both at the same moment from a high point in the leaning tower of Pisa. In theory both should fall at the same rate, and Galileo knew that, but the resistance of air made the result turn out differently as the wind made the feather behave like a parachute. The theoretical knowledge behind the experiment had broad ramifications and related to the greater work on gravity by Isaac Newton (1642–1727) many years later. For example, if the earth were rotating rather than remaining still as the church believed, anything dropped from the tower should fall behind it. Galileo was convinced of that but could not demonstrate it. At a very much later time, as astronauts reached the moon, the awareness that here was an environment with no air revived memories of Galileo. A decision was made to carry out his experiment and it was performed by David Scott and Jim Irwin on their Apollo 15 mission. True to Galileo's convictions both the feather and stone fell to the moon's surface at the same time. The event was filmed and is now available in most educational libraries.

The great turning point in Galileo's life was triggered by an insignificant event in another country, Holland, in 1608. A spectacle maker accidentally arranged some lenses so that they provided significant magnification of distant objects. Galileo heard about this shortly afterward and developed a similar result.

Up to that time, the telescope was not yet available and all observations of the skies came from naked eye vision. His first telescope was a simple handmade thing. He placed two lenses into a tube of lead, one on each end. Both lenses were plain on one side but convex and concave respectively on the other side, and with this instrument he was able to see a ninefold magnification of objects. This was the first telescope ever used for astronomical observations and before long it had completely and irreversibly changed age-old superstitions about the solar system. When Galileo arranged demonstrations for his scholarly friends and acquaintances they refused, again and again, to accept the evidence of the telescope. They were convinced that it was a trick, arranged by putting pictures inside the telescope. Galileo was so influenced by their behavior that, for a time, he would not believe what he saw through the telescope without repeating the viewing over and over again. At times, with objects at short range, he would look at them through the telescope, then examine them at close range to make sure that both appearances were identical.

As he gained confidence with the new instrument, Galileo began to use it to view the moon and the various planets of the solar system. Among the planets, Jupiter was one of the most prominent and usually the brightest. It was his observations of it on the nights of January 7–10, 1610, that changed the course of history. For the first time there was clear evidence confirming what Copernicus had

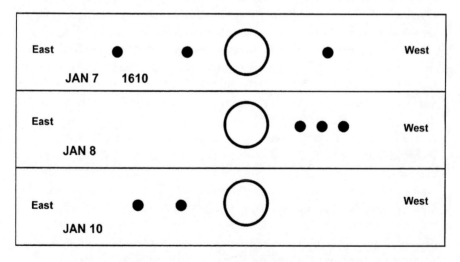

Figure 2.3. Galileo's observation of Jupiter's satellites using his telescope was the first time that a telescope was employed to observe planetary motions.

written, evidence that could easily be checked by anyone at any time. Figure 2.3 illustrates what Galileo saw. On January 7, there were three small stars close to Jupiter, but on the next night they had completely changed their positions. He could not view them on the evening of the ninth because of clouds, but when he looked again on January 10, they had changed again and one of them was missing. On each of the three nights, the so-called stars were equally spaced and all were in a straight line relative to Jupiter. Almost immediately Galileo realized what he was seeing. These were not stars but satellites circling around Jupiter just like the moon's orbit around the earth.

In spite of his strong confidence in the findings of Copernicus, Galileo was anxious to avoid controversy on the issue and decided not to reveal his discovery. Within a couple of years however, the news got out when a letter that Galileo had written to a friend was found and passed on to the church's leaders. In the letter Galileo asserted that every Biblical interpretation must be interpreted in the light of scientific findings, the very opposite of the church's position. Fortunately for Galileo, no one in the church's hierarchy thought that his statement was a problem because it was assumed that the church was right and good science would always agree with it. A few years later, Galileo wrote another letter in which he strongly attacked the ideas of Aristotle, pointing out that a non-literal interpretation of the Bible was essential when a literal rendering would clash with proven facts about the physical world. This letter went on to say that the Copernican theory defines a physical reality, namely that the sun is at the center of the solar system and does not move while the earth rotates on itself and also moves around the sun. This was too much for the church's authorities and the Pope appointed Bellarmine as the inquisitor to investigate the Copernican theory.

Under direction from Bellarmine the cardinals of the Inquisition met in 1616 and received evidence from their theological experts. Copernicus' teachings were condemned and Galileo told that he was forbidden to hold any of the condemned teachings. At this time, Galileo was about to publish his discoveries, so—knowing that a friend was about to become the next pope as Urban the Eighth—

decided to dedicate it to him. It was a dangerous game of politics and for a time it worked. The new Pope saw Galileo on several occasions and he assumed from these visits that his new discoveries would be acceptable to the church. He was quite wrong.

At this stage of his life, at 56, Galileo's health was poor. He began to work on his final treatise *Dialogue*, in 1624, and it took him six years to complete it. It was published in 1632 and dealt with the two views of the cosmos, the Ptolemaic and the Copernican. It was quickly banned by the church and Galileo was ordered to appear before the Inquisition in Rome. The charge against him was that he had violated the conditions laid down by the same Inquisition in 1616 when he was forbidden to hold the Copernican views of the cosmos.

The most interesting aspect of Galileo's trial comes from his defense by one of the church's leaders, Tommaso Campanella, someone who was convinced that the two books of God could not contradict each other (the heart of the issue in the conflict between biological evolution and creationism). Campanella's defense of Galileo is not only extraordinary because of his high standing in the church, but also because he defended the value of new discoveries in the cosmos strictly on the basis of Scriptural interpretations, not the evidence from scientists. His defense is concentrated on Galileo's argument that God is known in his works and in his word and these two books must support each other. Thus if any certainties in nature are discovered they ought to be utilized as aids in the true interpretation of the Bible. Campanella confirms this view. To him, while theology does not need proofs from science, it is strengthened by greater knowledge of the natural. He goes on to show how the Bible is full of injunctions about gaining knowledge of the natural world. God gave humans their five senses and a rational mind so that they might know his works better. Not to use these gifts would be as foolish as a man not using his feet to walk.

Campanella continues his support of Galileo with a series of Biblical quotations. He stresses that from the beginning, in Genesis, humans are found walking upright, facing the skies, unlike other animals which always look downwards toward the earth. Paul, in his letter to the Romans, points out that the invisible things about

God are known through the things he made. Human responsibility therefore is to observe the heavens and the earth out of curiosity so that knowledge is gained and humans thereby can fulfill their obligation to worship God. In Psalm 18, the Hebrew King David says that the heavens reveal the nature of God, and in Psalm 8 he announces his intention to gaze at the heavens, the contents of which were all shaped by the fingers of God. Hence, concludes Campanella, the work of astronomers is a happy and vital work. They bring the distant stars closer to people's eyes and reveal their secrets. More than to anyone else, the people are indebted to Galileo for this important work. Galileo's theory and the use of the telescope are now overwhelmingly accepted within Christian society. Therefore Campanella's philosophical theory has some merit.

BOOK OF GOD ONE **THE COSMOS**
BOOK OF GOD TWO **THE BIBLE**

THE TWO BOOKS OF GOD

Figure 2.4. Galileo's defense, like the Church's, was that the two books of God do not contradict each other. Problems arose over interpretations of the data derived from both books.

Despite Campanella's efforts to set him free, Galileo was treated as a heretic and accordingly condemned. The church authority that pronounced the verdict, the Inquisition, was more like a military tribunal than a court as would be understood today. It was an organ of repression and the humiliating process that accompanied a verdict was always a clear demonstration of its power. Galileo was required to kneel before the inquisitors and, with his hands on the Bible, swear that he believed all that is held, preached, and taught by the Holy Catholic and Apostolic Church. While in that posture he had to further declare that he would abandon the false opinion that the sun is the center of the world and is immovable and that the earth is not the center of the world and moves. He then added, among several other promises, that he abjured, cursed, and detested these errors and heresies. It is always hard when a person has to make false statements in order to save his life. That was what Galileo did because he knew very well that the statement about the earth and sun was wrong. As a reward he was condemned to lifelong house arrest instead of being burned at the stake. He lived for eight years after the verdict, experiencing oncoming blindness, and always under the watchful eye of the church authorities.

Newton and Burnet

In the second half of the seventeenth century, scientists made great strides in establishing their discoveries as integral parts of society, so much so that this period is known as the scientific revolution. Isaac Newton was the dominant figure and his ideas on gravity paved the way for the dramatic developments in space travel today. He has been described as one of the foremost scientific intellects of all time. He attended Cambridge University where his studies were interrupted for two years because the terrible plague which swept over London and surrounding areas at that time had spread to Cambridge. Newton was 23 when his studies were interrupted and he had to move back to his home in Lincolnshire, a hundred miles north of Cambridge. It was during the two years there, and at such a young age, that he wrote his best known work, *Principia,* a description of the principles of natural philosophy. Soon after he returned to Cambridge, he was appointed professor of Mathematics in which capacity he stayed for 27 years.

Like others of fame, there are apocryphal stories associated with Newton, such as the one about the apple falling from a tree, giving him new insights into the operation of gravity. Whatever the source of his first insight into that powerful force of nature, he developed it into a far wider sphere of application. He observed first that the higher the elevation from which an object fell, the faster it traveled on its way down. He called that feature the acceleration of gravity, extending it to distances in space and speculating that the orbit of the moon was a consequence of gravitational force. He illustrated this idea with reference to a cannon ball being projected from a cannon. If the force behind the ball is small it will travel a short distance and fall to earth. If however, the force is great enough to balance the downward pull of gravity the ball will be put into orbit around the earth. Through reasoning such as this Newton came to the conclusion that any two objects in space exert gravitational force on each other and he illustrated it as follows: M1D1 = M2D2. M is the mass of the object and d is the distance from each mass to the center of gravity or center of mass. This point is similar to the fulcrum on a see-saw, the point that balances the different weights on the ends.

Throughout the seventeenth century, the dominance of the church within a ubiquitous religious culture was a reality that Newton, like all others, had to face. He was far from being neutral in his attitude to it. England had come through a series of major changes after the death of Oliver Cromwell in 1660. Under the two kings, Charles the Second and James the Second, considerable unrest developed throughout the country with many fearing that the RCC would once again secure power. Finally, in 1688, William of Orange, a Dutch Protestant, took over the country and Protestantism was restored to the center of power. While Newton played no part in these events, they greatly affected his life and career. He was a committed Protestant, who always supported the Anglican Church and demonstrated an animosity toward Catholicism. These views gave him high status with the new royal family. It was in the time of Cromwell that Newton formed his personal religious philosophy, a Puritan outlook emphasizing the inerrancy of scripture, the role of the Bible as the sole source of religious truth, and the imminence of the world's end. For one who had gone so far in science, paving the way for much of the space travel challenges of our time, Newton's devotion to the Bible and his intensive studies of it are surprises.

He studied the Bible daily, believing it was true in every respect. All through his life he was always testing scientific findings against biblical truth and he never found any contradictions in so doing. He saw his scientific work as a method through which he could reinforce belief in the Bible. In his later years he devoted more and more of his time to Biblical research. Much of it was published. He felt that anyone who had the ability to explain the workings of the world and did not share it with all humanity was denying God one form of adoration. During the reign of James the Second, the King decided to change the universities into Catholic institutions. Newton entered politics, determined to fight against this change, and represented the University of Cambridge for some years. As Newtonian science became increasingly accepted all across Europe, Newton became the most highly esteemed natural philosopher of the century. His last years were spent in revising his major works and defending himself against critics.

He made a special study of Solomon's Temple, seeking to find out its dimensions. It remains a bit of a mystery why a scholar of his ability and fame should retain his early outlook on a literal interpretation of the Bible. Galileo and others had shown the inadequacy of the Biblical story of Noah's Flood. Yet, when Newton's friend Thomas Burnet had difficulty making the Biblical account fit science, Newton suggested a possible special miracle by God as the probable solution. It was another instance of the kind people have seen so often where deeply embedded dogmas override good judgment. Newton was not the only one to do this. The common element however in these men was their devotion to the truth of both books, Bible and nature. Unlike the church of Galileo's time or the creationists of today, science was their friend, not an enemy of truth.

Thomas Burnet was a contemporary of Newton and chaplain to the king of England. He was devoted to the traditional interpretation of the Bible. His publication *The Sacred Theory of the Earth*, in 1681, described Noah's flood as having covered the whole earth. Since he knew that the oceans of the world would not be sufficient for that purpose, he invoked the ancient Hebrew notion of vast stores of water beneath the earth which were released on to the surface to cause the flood. In his mind these subterranean supplies of water would equal the amount stored in nine oceans! Burnet chose 2 Peter 3: 5–6, quoted later in this chapter, as the foundation for his theory. His book was very popular in its time and was translated into several languages. For the purposes of this book, it is a good example of an ill advised intertwining of science and religion.

Burnet's relations with the prevailing religious culture were different from almost all the other scientists. He was loyal to it, unlike so many before him, and he was also deeply devoted to good science. While he was in sympathy with the prevailing Biblical views of the cosmos and the age of the earth, he did not always insist on literal accuracy. He conceded that the six days of creation might represent six periods of undetermined length rather than days as we understand them now. That particular concession was not acceptable to the King of England and it cost him his prestigious position as the King's private confessor. Burnet felt that the history of the earth is the result of unchanging natural laws and he saw his book as an accurate account that would fit both the theological and the scientific content of his times. Convinced as he was that truth was a unity, he could not imagine anything being discovered that would challenge his outlook. In his mind, as with Galileo, God was the author of both natural laws and the Bible, so these two books could not therefore contradict each other.

Burnet's work is doubly interesting. It represents a time when a serious scientist believed he could rationalize contemporary theological viewpoints with the frontiers of scientific discovery. The second reason for the importance of his work lies in the ways creationists frequently use the same reasoning as his to explain narratives such as Noah's flood. Scientists nowadays regard him as a fool who tried to impose dogmas of scriptural authority on scientific investigations. Some of the content in *The Sacred Theory of the Earth*, sound a bit familiar if one were to listen to the present-day arguments advanced by creationists. Burnet talks of the earth being about 5,000 years old, a popular concept at the present time with the young-earth creationists. His book also offers strong support for natural theology, now referred to as intelligent design, namely that the Biblical records give us evidence of both the Creator and of the initial form of the earth. Burnet's ideas about the materials of the primeval earth were that they had been precipitated from the initial chaos and later sorted according to their densities. Heavy rocks and metals formed the core with a liquid layer above; terrestrial materials and air were eventually precipitated to form a perfectly smooth, featureless surface, like that of an egg. Thus the original earth was smooth and beautiful, without faults and wrinkles of the type seen today.

In this smooth earth were the first scenes of the world, and the first generation of humanity. Burnet goes on to describe it as having the beauty of youth and the bloom of nature in its prime. There was not a wrinkle, scar, or fracture in any part of it. The climate of this ante-diluvial world was a perpetual spring. Then came Noah's flood and the ruined world as seen today was the result. The collapse of the crust into subterranean cavities occurred during the flood. The flood itself was the result of natural causes, Burnet argued, which culminated in the destruction of the world. When the flood waters had retreated into internal caverns, the earth had become "a gigantic and hideous ruin ... a broke and confused heap of bodies." The account of Noah's flood, which is regarded as having occurred 1,600 years after the creation of the earth, dominates the book. In Burnet's mind this flood covered the entire earth including the highest mountains.

He described the rains descending after an unusual manner, and the fountains of the great deep being broken open. A general destruction and devastation hit the earth and all things in it, including all of humanity and other living creatures except for Noah and his family. After the waters had raged for some time they began to lessen and shrink in volume. Finally they retired into their channels and caverns within the earth. Mountains and fields began to reappear and the whole earth came to life once again. From the little remnant preserved in the ark humanity and animal life as we know it today were propagated. In this way the old world perished and the present arose from its ruins and remains. Burnet saw it all, the earliest time in earth's history, Noah's flood, the present, and the future through the eyes of Peter as recorded in his second letter, chapter three, verses five to seven:

> They deliberately forget that long ago by God's word the heavens existed and the earth was formed out of water and by water. By these waters also the world of that time was deluged and destroyed. By the same word the present heavens and earth are reserved for fire, being kept for the day of judgment and destruction of ungodly men.

Burnet was also guided, in the light of his times, with a high respect for scientific discoveries and, as such, was a model for those in the present age who have difficulty harmonizing the Bible with established scientific theories. This was how Burnet explained the process. It is dangerous to use the authority of the Bible when confronted with new facts about the natural world. Rather, that is the occasion to reexamine one's interpretation of the Bible. Burnet was well-acquainted with his contemporary, Isaac Newton, and on one occasion Newton suggested that God might have made the earth rotate much more slowly in earlier times, thus producing days of enormous lengths. Burnet rejected this suggestion because he was so convinced that God worked according to fixed natural laws. He asked his friend how could he explain the speeding up of the earth's rotation much later without rejecting the idea of fixed laws. The conflicts between faith and fact, so well illustrated in Burnet's work, continued to appear in later years as did the violence of the church against heretics. Witches, always women, were burned at the stake in many parts of Europe as recently as the year 1700. Men who opposed the church's interpretations of the Bible were hanged.

All of this background is essential for an adequate understanding of contemporary creationism. Right up to the time of Darwin every scientist operated within a religious culture. There was no such thing as secular science. All the great scientists lived and worked as loyal members of the church, with many perceiving their discoveries as revelations of the work of their creator. It is difficult today to think of Newton or Hutton without including their theological views. Even as recently as 1850 Darwin battled with the relation of his work to religion. Asa Gray's views and Darwin's readings in Newman show that the age-old interaction was still going on at that time. The intensity of the conflicts that occurred only strengthens the creationists' arguments that notions of a supreme being have always been integral parts of good science. Why should they be excluded today? The answer of course is that these are important philosophical questions that need to be discussed, but they have nothing to do with science at the school level.

For more than a thousand years, until scientists like Copernicus and Galileo demonstrated their inadequacies, the church held dogmatically to ancient views of the cosmos that had nothing to do with its faith. Those very old understandings of the age of the earth and its relation to other parts of the cosmos were human constructs, limited by what was known and what was influenced by myths. During this long period of time, few people seemed able to distinguish between transcendental revelations of truth and facts about life on earth acquired through the normal use of the senses and the mind. Many creationists still retain a loyalty to ancient cosmology like the church's leaders of 600 years ago. Either they are incapable of distinguishing between revealed truth and ordinary human knowledge or they insist on retaining old interpretations of the Bible that are no longer tenable. Hence, when Darwin published his research findings, there was panic, even though they had nothing to do with the foundations of Christian faith. The lesson that all have to learn from the roots of creationism is to keep these two domains of understanding separate—faith and scientific facts.

THREE

The Impact of Science

In an age of computers and space travel, amid an explosion of scientific discoveries and with instruments that recognize—in real time—humankind's innermost processes of thought, it's very hard to imagine the impact of two revolutionary discoveries in the middle of the nineteenth century. These were times of staid, conservative patterns of thought. There had been little change for many centuries in the ways people thought about the earth and its history. Parents and grandparents shared the same ethical code and similar beliefs about the Bible, including the conviction that humans were recent, unique creations of God. Books and libraries confirmed their views. Into such an environment came two new spectacular views of the earth and its inhabitants: James Hutton's dating of the earth's age and Charles Darwin's revelation of the common ancestry in all life forms. No one had ever hinted previously that the earth was billions of years old or that humans had developed, just like all other living things, from simpler forms of life.

The shock effect of Hutton's and Darwin's discoveries was powerful. They shattered long standing social norms and their implications reverberated down the rest of the nineteenth century and into the twentieth. James Hutton's discovery was first circulated in 1788 but, because of opposition from other scholars, it was not widely recognized until the middle of the nineteenth century. Thus, almost simultaneously, two long standing assumptions about humans and their environment were challenged. From the earliest days of Christendom a fixed set of interpretations of the Bible had been enforced by an authoritative church. As we saw earlier, there was no freedom of thought. Daniel Boorstin in *The Discoverers: A*

History of Man's Search to Know His World and Himself, writes about the period 300 to 1300 AD as a Europe-wide phenomenon of scholarly amnesia.

Even after 1300 the threats of church inquisitions and the realities of so-called heretics being burned alive were sufficient to deter fresh thinking. The age-old interpretations, many of them including acceptance of the early chapters of Genesis as an accurate history of the earth and the rest of the universe, had changed very little by the time Darwin's bombshell descended on the western world. As recently as 1849, 21 years before his death, Charles Dickens wrote a book for his children about the life of Jesus. The book was not published in his lifetime at the request of the author. It finally appeared in Britain in the 1930s. The view of the Bible that it espoused would have fit perfectly into the prevailing views of the church a thousand years earlier.

Scientific discoveries, of course, had been going on for a long time before 1850, and a great deal of interaction had taken place between scientists. It was both the extraordinary nature of the two new discoveries along with their timing that made a huge and lasting impact on everyone. They influenced morality, which up to this point had been based on a certain interpretation of the Bible, and they affected understandings of human value and destiny. In the last quarter of the nineteenth century, understandably, books about the Bible began to appear, questioning its accuracy and reinterpreting its meaning. Traditionalists became increasingly alarmed. Scientific discoveries were seen as threats to the good life rather than aids. By the early twentieth century many of these traditionalists saw evolution as symbolizing immorality and an anti-god mentality. These ideas were to be reinforced later by additional scientific ideas resulting, as we will see, in the dramatic anti-evolution movements of the 1920s. For now, an example in greater detail of these mid-nineteenth century events follows.

James Hutton

The first of these developments was the awareness that the earth is a very, very old place, not the few thousand years that had been assumed. This finding dates back to an earlier point, toward the end of the previous century, when James Hutton, a Scottish physician and what was then called a gentleman farmer made an extraordinary discovery. Gentleman farmer means that he owned a farm, but that other people did all the necessary work on it, leaving him to follow other interests. He traveled widely throughout Britain, studying rocks and finding fossils in different layers of rocks. The prevailing view of his time about these fossils, a view that dated back to the early centuries of Christendom and was still being held by Hutton's contemporaries, attributed them to ancient violent upheavals of the surface of the earth. Hutton disagreed. Near his home on the east coast of Scotland he found successive layers of sandstone and shale, all of them either vertical or folded back on one another. He concluded that rivers must have eroded an ancient landscape, shifting tiny fragments of rock sediment down to the sea and compacting them into sedimentary rock.

Later, according to Hutton, these layers of sedimentary rock were uplifted and twisted into their present forms. Knowing that sedimentary rocks are formed by the processes of river and wind erosion which he observed taking place year by year, Hutton concluded that an enormous amount of time must have elapsed for the rock particles to be compacted into solid rock and then uplifted. He described his fresh awareness of the earth's great age in these words, "I see no vestige of a beginning and no prospect of an end." In *Theory of the Earth*, published in 1795, he wrote, "It is necessary that we change from measuring time by the clock in the church tower and look instead at the clock in the mountains." Hutton had no means of measuring the age of the earth. Techniques for dating rocks came later. Nevertheless, the science of geology was born as a result of his findings and he is known today as its founder. Like biology because of the discoveries of DNA and the Genome, geology today is a very different scientific field than it was in 1795. Tectonic plates and their relation to moving continents are now well-known phenomena and geologists can measure with accuracy the distances these plates move, year by year, using a global positioning system.

Like all scientists of his time, Hutton was a firm believer in the truths of the Bible. It is to his credit that he was willing to place his research in opposition to the accepted Biblical interpretation of his day that required a relatively young earth. Paradoxically, it was his belief in the Bible that inspired his research. He wanted to find out all he could about this world that his Creator had made. His findings, in his mind, perfectly fit his theology. The earth had been created for human habitation and now he finds, appropriately, that it is self-perpetuating. Though humans consume many vital elements, in the course of time they are all replenished. Animals use up oxygen and plants regenerated it by using the animal's carbon dioxide waste. Rain, so essential for human crops, is supplied continuously by the cycling of water. Even coal is regenerated through the burying and consolidation of plants that had earlier captured energy from the sun. As a farmer Hutton knew that soil is lost as a result of erosion, but then it is renewed through geological uplift and the subsequent breakdown of rock.

The concept of uniformitarianism emerged from Hutton's work. By this term it is asserted that the changes we see as having occurred in the past were caused by the activities of rivers, wind, temperature changes, and gravity, all of them working in the same way and a similar pace as we see today. Catastrophic events also occurred over the billions of years of earth's existence, some of them very destructive, but in terms of the amount of time involved, they were only momentary. Unfortunately, a much more influential scholar in France by the name of Georges Cuvier was devoted to the older view of earth's history, that all changes happen as a result of a series of catastrophes and that what appears to be a great deal of time is, in fact, the result of catastrophes which caused huge changes in short periods of time. Cuvier opposed Hutton's new theory of the age of the earth and, because he was able to resist it for a very long time, it was close to the middle of the nineteenth century before Hutton's work received the universal acclaim to which it was entitled.

For Hutton, God had built a great clock-type machine, a world composed of endless cycles without beginning or end, because presumably he saw his Creator as having no beginning or end. Evolution, as we know it today, did not exist for him. Charles Lyell, the

British Geologist, picked up Hutton's concept of uniformitarianism and popularized it in his *Principles of Geology* about 40 years after Hutton's death. He also showed that the relative ages of the different layers of rock could be determined by the proportions they yielded of shells from living and extinct types of molluscs. Lyell was one of the most influential geologists of all time. He gave us the names Pliocene, Miocene, and Eocene, present day epochs of the Cenozoic Era. His close association with—and his great influence on—Charles Darwin may be of even greater significance. Lyell's second edition of *Principles of Geology* had just been published as Darwin was on the Beagle off the west coast of South America. A copy of the book was

EON	ERA	PERIOD	
Phanerozoic	Cenozoic *Mammals* *Birds*	Quaternary	0.01
		Tertiary	65
	Mesozoic *Reptiles*	Cretaceous	144
		Jurassic	208
		Triassic	245
	Paleozoic *Fish*	Permian	286
		Carboniferous	360
		Devonian	408
		Silurian	438
		Ordovician	505
		Cambrian	570
Proterozoic 2500	**Geological Time Chart**		
Archaean 4600	**Numbers represent millions of years ago**		

Figure 3.1. This geological chart shows when different forms of life appeared. It is based on Charles Lyell's *Principles of Geology*, a book that helped Charles Darwin during his voyages on the Beagle.

sent to him and he read it eagerly throughout the voyage. It contained the data on shells from different species in different layers. Strangely, in spite of this information, Lyell maintained the older catastrophe view of earth's history until Darwin's book was published.

Charles Darwin

The other great discovery of the mid-nineteenth century, Darwin's *Origin of Species*, became a great source for the evolution debate. While the word *evolution* was rarely used by Darwin, his name and the adjective *Darwinism* has been inseparably linked with evolution for more than 100 years. The principal opposition to Darwin was not so much the notion of earlier forms of life having developed from previous forms, but the explanations suggested for the evolving process. These were the things that offended people because they implied in the popular mind both the absence of a creator and the rejection of biblical accounts as false. As discussed in the next chapter, new ideas have been advanced to explain the process of evolution but these were not in evidence in the early part of the twentieth century. A look at Darwin's introduction to *The Origin of Species* as published in 1859 will help secure a clear picture of his conclusions and, at the same time, the ways in which a scientist works.

> When on board H.M.S. *Beagle*, as naturalist, I was much struck with certain facts in the distribution of the inhabitants of South America, and in the geological relations of the present to the past inhabitants of that continent. These facts seemed to me to throw some light on the origin of species—that mystery of mysteries, as it has been called by one of our greatest philosophers. On my return home, it occurred to me, in 1837, that something might perhaps be made out on this question by patiently accumulating and reflecting on all sorts of facts which could possibly have any bearing on it. After five years' work I allowed myself to speculate on the subject, and drew up some short notes; these I enlarged in 1844 into a sketch of the conclusions, which then seemed to me probable: from that period

to the present day I have steadily pursued the same object. I hope that I may be excused for entering on these personal details, as I give them to show that I have not been hasty in coming to a decision.

My work is now nearly finished; but as it will take me two

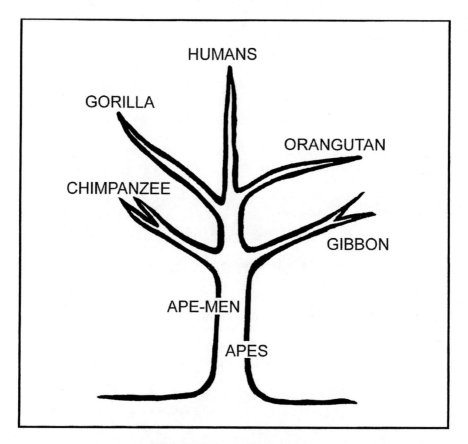

HUMAN PEDIGREE
ACCORDING TO DARWIN

Figure 3.2. Charles Darwin, who was not an expert on the mechanisms that cause changes in life forms, thought that they happened in a linear sequence such as from ape-men directly to humans. The science of cladistics has shown the inadequacy of this view.

or three more years to complete it, and as my health is far from strong, I have been urged to publish this Abstract. I have more especially been induced to do this, as Mr. Wallace, who is now studying the natural history of the Malay archipelago, has arrived at almost exactly the same general conclusions that I have on the origin of species. Last year he sent to me a memoir on this subject, with a request that I would forward it to Sir Charles Lyell, who sent it to the Linnean Society, and it is published in the third volume of the journal of that Society. Sir C. Lyell and Dr Hooker, who both knew of my work—the latter having read my sketch of 1844—honoured me by thinking it advisable to publish, with Mr. Wallace's excellent memoir, some brief extracts from my manuscripts. This Abstract, which I now publish, must necessarily be imperfect. I cannot here give references and authorities for my several statements; and I must trust to the reader reposing some confidence in my accuracy. No doubt errors will have crept in, though I hope I have always been cautious in trusting to good authorities alone.

I can here give only the general conclusions at which I have arrived, with a few facts in illustration, but which, I hope, in most cases will suffice. No one can feel more sensible than I do of the necessity of hereafter publishing in detail all the facts, with references, on which my conclusions have been grounded; and I hope in a future work to do this. For I am well aware that scarcely a single point is discussed in this volume on which facts cannot be adduced, often apparently leading to conclusions directly opposite to those at which I have arrived. A fair result can be obtained only by fully stating and balancing the facts and arguments on both sides of each question; and this cannot possibly be here done. I much regret that want of space prevents my having the satisfaction of acknowledging the generous assistance which I have received from very many naturalists, some of them personally unknown to me. I cannot, however, let this opportunity pass without expressing my deep obligations to Dr Hooker, who for the last fifteen years has aided me in every possible way by his large stores of knowledge and his excellent judgment.

In considering the Origin of Species, it is quite conceivable that a naturalist, reflecting on the mutual affinities of organic beings, on their embryological relations, their geographical distribution, geological succession, and other such facts, might come to the conclusion that each species had not been independently created, but had descended, like varieties, from other species. Nevertheless, such a conclusion, even if well founded, would be unsatisfactory, until it could be shown how the innumerable species inhabiting this world have been modified so as to acquire that perfection of structure and co-adaptation which most justly excites our admiration. Naturalists continually refer to external conditions, such as climate, food, &c., as the only possible cause of variation. In one very limited sense, as we shall hereafter see, this may be true; but it is preposterous to attribute to mere external conditions, the structure, for instance, of the woodpecker, with its feet, tail, beak, and tongue, so admirably adapted to catch insects under the bark of trees. In the case of the mistletoe, which draws its nourishment from certain trees, which has seeds that must be transported by certain birds, and which has flowers with separate sexes absolutely requiring the agency of certain insects to bring pollen from one flower to the other, it is equally preposterous to account for the structure of this parasite, with its relations to several distinct organic beings, by the effects of external conditions, or of habit, or of the volition of the plant itself.

The author of the "Vestiges of Creation" would, I presume, say that, after a certain unknown number of generations, some bird had given birth to a woodpecker, and some plant to the mistletoe, and that these had been produced perfect as we now see them; but this assumption seems to me to be no explanation, for it leaves the case of the coadaptations of organic beings to each other and to their physical conditions of life, untouched and unexplained. It is, therefore, of the highest importance to gain a clear insight into the means of modification and coadaptation. At the commencement of my observations it seemed to me probable that a careful study of domesticated animals and of cultivated plants would offer the best chance of making out this obscure problem. Nor have I been disappointed; in this and in all other perplexing cases I have invariably found that our knowledge, imperfect though it be, of variation under domestication, afforded the best and safest clue. I may venture to express my conviction of the high value of such studies, although they have been very commonly neglected by naturalists.

Evolution and Creationism in the Public Schools

From these considerations, I shall devote the first chapter of this Abstract to Variation under Domestication. We shall thus see that a large amount of hereditary modification is at least possible, and, what is equally or more important, we shall see how great is the power of man in accumulating by his Selection successive slight variations. I will then pass on to the variability of species in a state of nature; but I shall, unfortunately, be compelled to treat this subject far too briefly, as it can be treated properly only by giving long catalogues of facts. We shall, however, be enabled to discuss what circumstances are most favourable to variation. In the next chapter the Struggle for Existence amongst all organic beings throughout the world, which inevitably follows from their high geometrical powers of increase, will be treated of. This is the doctrine of Malthus, applied to the whole animal and vegetable kingdoms. As many more individuals of each species are born than can possibly survive; and as, consequently, there is a frequently recurring struggle for existence, it follows that any being, if it vary however slightly in any manner profitable to itself, under the complex and sometimes varying conditions of life, will have a better chance of surviving, and thus be naturally selected. From the strong principle of inheritance, any selected variety will tend to propagate its new and modified form.

This fundamental subject of Natural Selection will be treated at some length in the fourth chapter; and we shall then see how Natural Selection almost inevitably causes much Extinction of the less improved forms of life and induces what I have called Divergence of Character. In the next chapter I shall discuss the complex and little known laws of variation and of correlation of growth. In the four succeeding chapters, the most apparent and gravest difficulties on the theory will be given: namely, first, the difficulties of transitions, or understanding how a simple being or a simple organ can be changed and perfected into a highly developed being or elaborately constructed organ; secondly the subject of Instinct, or the mental powers of animals; thirdly, Hybridism, or the infertility of species and the fertility of varieties when intercrossed; and fourthly, the imperfection of the Geological Record. In the next chapter I shall consider the geological succession of organic beings throughout time; in the eleventh and twelfth, their geographical distribution throughout space; in the thirteenth, their classification or mutual affinities, both when mature and in an embryonic condition. In the last chapter I shall give a brief recapitulation of the whole work, and a few concluding remarks.

No one ought to feel surprise at much remaining as yet unexplained in regard to the origin of species and varieties, if he makes due allowance for our profound ignorance in regard to the mutual relations of all the beings which live around us. Who can explain why one species ranges widely and is very numerous, and why another allied species has a narrow range and is rare? Yet these relations are of the highest importance, for they determine the present welfare, and, as I believe, the future success and modification of every inhabitant of this world. Still less do we know of the mutual relations of the innumerable inhabitants of the world during the many past geological epochs in its history. Although much remains obscure, and will long remain obscure, I can entertain no doubt, after the most deliberate study and dispassionate judgment of which I am capable, that the view which most naturalists entertain, and which I formerly entertained—namely, that each species has been independently created—is erroneous. I am fully convinced that species are not immutable; but that those belonging to what are called the same genera are lineal descendants of some other and generally extinct species, in the same manner as the acknowledged varieties of any one species are the descendants of that species. Furthermore, I am convinced that Natural Selection has been the main but not exclusive means of modification.

These eight paragraphs from Darwin's introduction provide an excellent example of the way a scientist works. It's similar to the outline in Chapter One of John Dewey's work. The differences between the school classroom and the research scientist is only a matter of scale, the level at which scientific work is carried on. The process is always the same. Look at Darwin's first paragraph. Darwin began with a puzzle arising naturally from his visit to South America, step one in scientific inquiry. He followed up on the puzzle after returning home, searching for any information that might cast light on it. This quest continued for five years, quite a long period of time for step two, accumulating data to increase his knowledge of related things. He knew he was engaged in a big idea and so he wanted to make sure he was on the right track. Finally, as can be seen in his first paragraph, he came to some tentative theories, what are called hypotheses, about the reasons for the puzzle. This is what is called step three in Dewey's scientific method.

Darwin's second paragraph describes his following up on his hypotheses, first by comparing his notes with the work of two close friends, Wallace and Lyell, who had been working on puzzles that were similar to his. As mentioned, he had been reading Lyell's latest book while on the Beagle. He then went on to put his ideas in writing and then published them in order to test them out as fully as possible with a large number of scientists. This is a good example of step four, the testing out of hypotheses in new situations. At the end of the paragraph there is a valuable statement about the possibilities of errors. Every good scientist is aware of these possibilities and the reason for circulating ideas widely is to make sure that if there are errors they will be found before conclusions are drawn. Hypotheses never become conclusions, or theories which are the same thing in science, until they have been thoroughly tested out and found true in many different settings.

In paragraphs three and four, Darwin is seen to be willing to debate his findings with anyone who might have a different set of data. This is a commendable extra to what has been already done about testing hypotheses. He goes on to list some of the possible alternative views that some might hold. Finally, toward the end of his introduction he affirmed that his findings confirm his theory that all forms of life came from a simple original form. He also suggested that natural selection would be the mechanism by which the different life forms were transformed into new species but he allowed for other mechanisms. This is the final and fifth stage of the scientific method and clearly Darwin went to much effort to test out all his ideas before coming to a firm conclusion. Paradoxically, at this time in which Darwin was opening up the world of science to new and fascinating prospects, the Roman Catholic Church decided to extend its historic authoritarianism. Pope Pius the Ninth decreed two new doctrines—papal infallibility and the Immaculate

Conception, that is to say, Mary was a virgin without sin. Both of these doctrines persist today.

Impact of Darwin's Work

Throughout the latter part of the nineteenth century and all of the twentieth, the central theme of Darwin's work has never been in doubt. It states that all organisms living on the earth today are descended from a common ancestry. This includes human life because there was no reason to think that the evolution of the human body from those earlier forms was any different than the evolutionary processes in other forms of life. The only thing that changed since 1859 was a steady growth in evidence confirming the truth of the original idea. The one process suggested by Darwin for these changes is commonly known as natural selection. That is to say, the only agency at work in causing these changes through these billions of years were changes in the natural elements—the rocks, the wind, the temperature, the water, the food supply and so on—all acting on whatever inherited characteristics were received from earlier species.

It is essential to keep these two views of evolution separate, the reality of common descent and the mechanisms involved in the changes that occurred. One of the known facts from research findings that paralleled those of Darwin was the awareness that some species are more closely related to one another than they are to more distant relatives. They share more characteristics. This is the basis for medical research today as the search for cures is first carried out in mice or rats. At the same time common characteristics are now identified in all forms of life, thanks to DNA knowledge. There are however, as we would expect, fewer commonalities found as ties with earlier forms of life are examined, thus evincing a hierarchy of groups within groups. It is necessary, in the context of the evolution-creationism debate, to add that scientific research always proceeds by trying to disprove, not prove ideas and hypotheses. As evidence accumulates that an idea cannot be disproved, even when tested out in many different environments, its reliability steadily increases.

Evolution and Creationism in the Public Schools

The massive and normative evidence for evolution comes from the history of life embedded in rocks, the fossils. While for any one period of time the volume of fossils available or even discoverable may be few—igneous and metamorphic rocks destroy all the fossils they touch—nevertheless the total volume presently available is immense. They are found in sedimentary formations, former lakes and oceans, and they have been discovered in rocks almost as old as the earth. The earth's age is known to be more than four billion years, a figure calculated from several different sources. In Australia, remains of bacteria were found in rocks three and a half billion years old. Bacteria are far simpler in their DNA structure than any one of all the known forms of life past or present. In terms of evolution one would expect that their fossils would be found in earth's oldest sedimentary rocks.

Darwin, like Hutton, grew up in a society that interpreted earth and human history from the biblical statements. He could easily have entered the Anglican ministry because that was a profession frequently selected by relatively-wealthy families like his and at one point it was suggested for him. Instead, he studied biology. When he was 50 years of age, bad health forced him to take time away from work. There were doubts and questions already in his mind, particularly objections to ideas about eternal rewards or punishments for earthly deeds, so he spent some time studying several major theological works. Around the same time, his 10-year-old daughter became seriously ill. Darwin visited her at the hospital day after day. After a month, she died and he was heartbroken. He wrote a friend saying, "God knows we can neither see on any side a gleam of comfort." This frame of mind, notions of an unknown god who cannot be kind and loving because he did not save his daughter's life was reinforced later in biological study. He could not for instance imagine a loving god designing the ichneumonid wasp which lays its eggs on a caterpillar. When the eggs hatch, they eat their still-living host.

Darwin often said he wished he could see evidence of design and kindness in the environment within which he worked so that he could believe in God. He was a true scientist in this aspect of his life, insisting on evidence for belief. He was fully aware of the beauty of nature, especially of humanity, and was offended by the idea that brute force could be responsible for it all. Asa Gray, a colleague at Harvard University with whom he first shared his ideas on the origins of species, tried unsuccessfully to persuade him that God was responsible for all of it. He did not succeed and Darwin came to the conclusion that the design of the universe is too big a subject for the human intellect. He explained it as natural forces operating by chance, in other words natural selection. He knew about many of the laws operating in biology and so proposed that everything must be the result of the operations of the biosphere's natural laws, both the good ones and the bad.

Fundamentalism

These two discoveries of the nineteenth century carried echoes of threat all through the first two decades of the twentieth century. To those who felt that their biblical convictions were being violated, with consequent damage to public morals, the threat loomed larger and larger with the passage of time. Shortly before World War I, conservative Christians came together and published a series of booklets, "The Fundamentals," designed to reaffirm the authority and trustworthiness of the Bible. The term fundamentalism, referring to the philosophy espoused by the authors of these booklets, came into use in the years that followed. Articles on science and Christian faith affirmed that whatever evolutionary views might be held by people, God's creative power working within organisms was the cause. Other articles insisted that new species could only evolve within certain groups. Humanity, in particular, must be seen as a special creation of God. It was not long before new and greater threats to conservatism appeared. Immediately after World War I, almost overnight as it were, three new developments profoundly changed the status quo in both Europe and the United States.

Before going into the details of these developments, it is necessary to consider the aftermath of World War I. It brought Europe, the part of the world that had been the pinnacle of western civilization, into deep degradation. The enormity of the four-year slaughter that took place was later referred to as the horrors of all the ages being inflicted on armies and civilians alike. Five million soldiers died and an additional twenty million were injured. The dead and wounded were left where they fell. Starvation was used as a weapon to force surrender and poison gas, against all the understandings of international law, was employed across the trenches on the western front. It would be hard to exaggerate the extent to which this war to end all wars, as it was called, had permanently affected peoples' outlook on life. Brutality and social disintegration had become commonplace events.

Within a year of the war's ending came the ideas of Sigmund Freud and Albert Einstein. The latter's theory of relativity of 1919 was an updating of the laws affecting gravity and light within the solar system. But in the popular mind, in spite of all Einstein's attempts to correct the error, they were interpreted as relativism. No longer in the popular mind were there moral absolutes. Everything was relative. Alongside this idea came Freud's contribution to scientific thought. His writings dated from the beginning of the twentieth century, particularly his 1900 publication *The Interpretation of Dreams*, but it was only in the fertile, disturbed society of the post war years that his ideas took root. He described religion and conscience as merely human concepts. Across North America, social norms gave way to rampant individualism, reinforced by the writings of authors such as James Joyce and D. H. Lawrence.

Young people no longer cared whether or not their behavior was acceptable to the adult norms. Traditionalists felt that everything valuable was rapidly eroding and so it seemed. Jazz had taken over, prohibition was ignored, and youth was enthralled with modern art, Freudian ideas, and the literature that focused on revealing everything about the personal inner life. To fundamentalists as well as among many other traditionalists, the time had come to put a stop to all this social decay. They were still convinced that Darwin's theory of evolution had been the root cause of all the social disruption of the previous hundred years and their convictions were reinforced by a third post–World War I development, the appearance of a godless Marxist government in Russia. Marxism was founded on the idea of class warfare, a viewpoint strongly influenced by Darwin's original comments about the survival of the fittest. Helped by a wave of revivalism, especially in the South, fundamentalists launched an attack across America on all references to evolution in the biological curricula of schools.

Their opposition was concentrated, just as another version of the same is done today by creationists, in the political life of the country. As covered in the introduction, no fewer than 37 bills opposing evolution were introduced in state legislatures in the 1920s. Many of them passed into law, declaring the teaching of evolution to be illegal. In the same period of time, half of all the published texts in biology made no reference to evolution. The fundamentalists were clearly winning. Indeed, given the overwhelming public support for creationism, they would win just as strongly today were it not for the huge volume of evidence now supporting evolution. Not very much of this evidence was available to legislatures in the early 1920s. Furthermore, fundamentalist thinking dominated much of the country at this time, especially the South, and this same thinking was therefore dominant among the members of legislatures.

Tennessee was the first to enact into law an act forbidding the teaching of evolution in all public educational institutions: "It shall be unlawful for any teacher in any of the Universities, Normals and all other public schools of the State which are supported in whole or in part by the public school funds of the State, to teach any theory that denies the story of the Divine Creation of man as taught in the Bible, and to teach instead that man has descended from a lower order of animals." It was enacted on May 13, 1925 and the first opposition to the new law followed soon after. A group of scientists, inspired by the American Civil Liberties Union, decided to test it in the courts whenever a suitable case presented itself. They knew quite well that the odds were heavily loaded against them. The people of the state were in favor of the new law as were many of the members of the legislature and the legal system. The jury would almost certainly be selected from local people. Given these conditions, their expectation was that they would lose the case and they would thus be able to appeal it to the U.S. Supreme Court where they could expect a more favorable decision. As will be seen, they were denied that important further step by a small, technical legal problem. As a result, in the public mind, the trial was a success for the Tennessee law and other legislatures were encouraged to pass similar legislation.

John Scopes Trial

Within a month of the Tennessee law being passed, John Thomas Scopes, a young high school biology teacher in Dayton, Tennessee (a small town of about 2,000), was arrested for violating an act of the state legislature by teaching evolution in his school. This was the opportunity the scientists were waiting for. They decided to defend Scopes and were able to secure the help of Clarence Darrow, a famous criminal lawyer, who offered to defend Scopes without a fee. On the prosecution's side was a three-time former presidential democratic candidate, William Jennings Bryan. Bryan, at 65, was closely identified with traditionalism, particularly with fundamentalist Christianity. In 1924 he drafted legislation to prevent the teaching of Darwinist evolutionary theory in Florida's public schools. His ability as a powerful speaker made him a popular choice for the World Christian Fundamental Association which asked him to assist with the case. His support for the anti-evolution law was motivated more by loyalty to public opinion than by the merits of the case.

William Jennings Bryan, three-time Democratic candidate for president and a populist, had been leading a fundamentalist crusade to banish Darwin's theory of evolution from American classrooms. Bryan's motivation for mounting the crusade is unclear. It is possible that Bryan, who cared deeply about equality, worried that Darwin's theories were being used by supporters of a growing eugenics movement that was advocating sterilization of "inferior stock." More likely, the Great Commoner came to his cause out of a concern that the teaching of evolution would undermine traditional values. Dayton was an extremely conservative community. It would be hard to find a single person in it who didn't subscribe to the documents written by the fundamentalists 20 years earlier. They were convinced that the literal interpretation of the Bible was the only way to approach it. A carnival atmosphere pervaded all of

Dayton as the opening of the trial approached. Banners of all kinds decorated the streets.

The court case, which became known internationally as the Monkey Trial, began in Dayton on July 11, 1925. A large number of reporters attends the trial, and probably every newspaper in America reported on it. Over 100 journalists arrived for the opening day. The *Chicago Tribune* installed its own radio transmitter and so the Monkey Trial became the first in American history to be broadcast to the nation. Three of Scopes' students were brought in as witnesses to his teaching of evolution. Nearly 1,000 people, 300 of whom were standing, jammed the county courthouse. A jury of 12 men, including 10 farmers, was quickly selected and proceedings then adjourned for the weekend. On the following Sunday, William Jennings Bryan delivered the sermon at Dayton's Methodist church. He used the occasion to attack the defense strategy in the Scopes case. As Bryan spoke, Judge Raulston and his entire family listened attentively from their front pew seats. As the trial continued on the next day, Raulston expressed concern that the courtroom floor might collapse from the weight of the many spectators. He then moved all proceedings to the lawn outside. The crowd by this time numbered more than 5,000.

Both sides in their opening remarks pictured the event as a struggle between good and evil, between truth and ignorance. Defense and prosecuting attorneys alike agreed that if evolution were to win, Christianity had to go. One of the first actions of the prosecution was to request the court to take note of the King James version of the Bible which was already present at the courthouse. John Scopes had already admitted responsibility for teaching evolution, using the text *Hunter's Civic Biology* in the process. Chief Prosecutor Tom Stewart then asked seven students in Scope's class a series of questions about his teachings. They all testified that Scopes told them that man and all other mammals had evolved from one-celled organisms. Bryan's only extended speech of the whole trial came on this second day in response to expert evidence in favor of evolution which the defense team presented. He complained that the evolutionists had humans descending from monkeys, and not even American ones at that, but rather only old world ones.

The highlight of the whole 11-day trial was Darrow's questioning of Bryan and I am including some of it here simply because the same questions could usefully be presented to many creationists today. On the seventh day of trial, Raulston asked the defense if it had any more evidence. What followed was what the *New York Times* described as "the most amazing court scene in Anglo-Saxon history." William Jennings Bryan was called to the stand as an expert on the Bible. Bryan, who began his testimony calmly, stumbled badly under Darrow's persistent questioning. At one point the exasperated Bryan said, "I do not think about things I don't think about." Darrow asked, "Do you think about the things you do think about?" Bryan responded, to the derisive laughter of spectators, "Well, sometimes." Both old warriors grew testy as the examination continued. The confrontation between Bryan and Darrow was reported by the press as a defeat for Bryan. According to one historian, "As a man and as a legend, Bryan was destroyed by his testimony that day." His performance was described as that of "a pitiable, punch drunk warrior."

Darrow Questioning Bryan

Q: You have given considerable study to the Bible, haven't you, Mr. Bryan. **A:** Yes, sir, I have tried to.

Q: The Bible says Joshua commanded the sun to stand still for the purpose of lengthening the day, doesn't it, and you believe it. **A:** I do.

Q: Do you believe at that time the entire sun went around the earth? **A:** No, I believe that the earth goes around the sun.

Q: Do you believe that the men who wrote it thought that the day could be lengthened or that the sun could be stopped? **A:** I don't know what they thought.

Q: You don't know? **A:** I think they wrote the fact without expressing their own thoughts.

Q: Can you answer my question directly? If the day was lengthened by stopping either the earth or the sun, it must have been the earth? **A** Well, I should say so.

Q: Now, Mr. Bryan, have you ever pondered what would have happened to the earth if it had stood still? **A:** No.

Q: You have not? **A:** No, the God I believe in could have taken care of that.

Q: I see. Have you ever pondered what would naturally happen to the earth if it stood still suddenly? **A:** No.

Q: You believe the story of the flood to be a literal interpretation? **A:** Yes, sir.

Q: When was that flood? **A:** I would not attempt to fix the date.

Q: Have you any idea how old the earth is? **A:** No.

Q: The book you have introduced in evidence tells you, doesn't it? **A:** I don't think it does.

Q: Let's see whether it does; is this the one? **A:** That is the one.

Q: It says B.C. 4004? **A:** That is Bishop Usher's calculation.

Q: That is printed in the Bible you introduced? **A:** Yes, sir.

Q: Would you say that the earth was only 4,000 years old? **A:** I think it is much older than that.

Q: Do you think the earth was made in six days? **A:** Not six days of 24 hours.

Q: Do you believe that the first woman was Eve? **A:** Yes.

Q: Do you believe she was literally made out of Adams's rib? **A:** I do.

Q: I am going to read a passage from the Bible: "And the Lord God said unto the serpent, because thou hast done this, thou art cursed above all cattle, and above every beast of the field; upon thy belly shalt thou go and dust shalt thou eat all the days of thy life." Do you think that is why the serpent is compelled to crawl upon its belly? **A:** I believe that.

Q: Do you believe the story of Jonah and the whale, that the whale swallowed Jonah and kept him alive for 3 days? **A:** Yes.

As the trial was nearly over. Darrow asked the jury to return a verdict of guilty. He knew that his client had little chance of winning so his hope lay in appealing the verdict to the Tennessee Supreme Court. The jury complied with Darrow's request, and Judge Raulston fined him $100. Under Tennessee law, Bryan was thereby denied the opportunity to deliver the closing speech on which he had labored for weeks. For all practical purposes it seemed that Scopes was guilty and evolution had won. However, within a year, the Tennessee Supreme Court reversed the decision of the Dayton court on a technicality. The fine should have been set by the jury, not the judge. Rather than send the case back for a new trial, the Tennessee Supreme Court decided to dismiss the case because it felt that nothing would be gained by such action.

The Scopes trial did not end the debate over the teaching of evolution, but it did represent a significant setback for the fundamentalists. Of the 15 states with anti-evolution legislation pending in 1925, only two, Arkansas and Mississippi, enacted laws restricting the teaching of evolution. At the same time, simply because the supporters of evolution lost their case, there was a reluctance in other states to challenge similar laws. Not until the shock of the Russian Sputnik satellite in 1957 were there serious reversals for those who still tried to banish evolution from the schools. On May 17, 1967, 42 years after the original law was passed, Tennessee repealed its anti-evolution law of May 13, 1925. A year later, as was noted at the end of Chapter One, Arkansas launched the first of many subsequent court actions to include either evolution or creationism in school classrooms.

The 1968 breakthrough case in Arkansas is described in Chapter One. Arkansas was in court again in 1981 defending an act of its legislature that was designed to provide equal time in science classrooms for biological evolution and creationism. It came to be known as Scopes Two because of the many similarities between the two cases. It was appealed by teachers and others and Federal Judge William Overton heard the appeal. His decision was a firm rejection of the act because it violated the Establishment Clause of the First Amendment of the U.S. Constitution and as part of his decision he added several valuable observations. These additional remarks have been effectively used as precedents in subsequent court cases making the 1981 decision a landmark case in the defense of the rights of teachers.

The State of Arkansas's Act 590 required schools to give balanced treatment to creation-science (CS) and evolution-science (ES). Balanced treatment meant equal time in classes, in textbook materials, in library resources, and in any other relevant educational programs. CS was defined, among other things, as scientific evidences and related inferences that indicate the sudden creation of the universe, energy, and life from nothing, and the earth's geology as caused by catastrophism, including the occurrence of a world wide flood. ES was defined, among other things, as scientific evidences and related inferences that indicate the emergence by naturalistic processes of the universe from disordered matter, and the emergence of life from non-life, and the inception of the earth and life several billion years ago.

The bill that became Act 590 had been introduced by Senator James Holsted in the Arkansas Senate, and was supported by the Rev. Blount, pastor of a church in Little Rock and Chairman of the Greater Little Rock Evangelical Fellowship. Holsted did not consult the State Department of Education, scientists, science teachers, or the Arkansas Attorney General before introducing the bill. In both the House of Representatives and the Senate the bill was only briefly discussed. There was no representation from either the scientific community or the State's Department of Education. In court, the plaintiffs claimed that, in addition to its violation of the Establishment Clause, it took away the rights of Arkansas teachers. Among the clauses that Judge Overton identified in the First Amendment was this one: No state can pass laws which aid one religion, aid all religions, or prefer one religion over another.

As he considered the plaintiffs' challenge, Judge Overton noted that the content of Act 590 was in keeping with the anti-evolution sentiment that had been influencing the teaching of biology in public schools between the 1920s and the 1960s. He linked it to the various manifestations of the fundamentalism that emerged in America at the end of the nineteenth century, based on a literal interpretation of the Bible and a belief in its inerrancy. These were the people, he said, who initiated a statute in Arkansas in 1929 which prohibited the teaching of evolution in public schools, and these were the ones who introduced scientific creationism in the 1960s as a more sophisticated anti-evolution tactic. Various organizations have emerged since that time, he added, to promote the idea that the Book of Genesis was supported by scientific data. Among these organizations are the Institute for Creation Research, the Creation Science Research Center, and the Creation Research Society.

Judge Overton went on to commend the Biological Sciences Curriculum Study (BSCS) as a model science curriculum for schools. BSCS was one of the curriculum projects funded by the National Science Foundation in the wake of the launch of the Soviet satellite Sputnik in order to raise academic standards in biology. It was designed by teams of scientists and teachers and it used the methods of John Dewey. More than half of all high school students studying biology today use the BSCS materials in one form or another. The theory of evolution is a fundamental part of all BSCS content. While referring to biology, Judge Overton pointed out that creationists' emphasis on origins is misplaced because it never forms part of the theory of evolution. Furthermore, because the theory of evolution begins with the existence of life and examines how it evolved, it cannot presuppose the absence or presence of a creator. Creationists' statements about evolution, he said, are a hodgepodge of limited assertions, many of which are quite inaccurate. The essential characteristics of any science, he concluded, are, (1) it is guided by natural law; (2) it is explained by reference to natural law; (3) it is testable against the empirical world; (4) its conclusions are tentative; (5) it is falsifiable. Creation science fails to meet these essential characteristics.

FOUR

How Do
Organisms Evolve?

From the time it was first enunciated in 1859, Darwin's basic proposition that all forms of life came from a common ancestry has never been seriously questioned. With the passage of time, that original statement was confirmed again and again. The problems that followed Darwin's work was the explanation he gave for the mechanisms causing change. In his view it was natural selection, or to put it in plain terms, competition among organisms for reproductive success would determine who survived and who became extinct in the long course of time. Darwin recognized from the beginning that there were probably other factors that affected the transitions from species to species, but his emphasis remained strongly oriented toward survival through competition. He of course was limited by the available knowledge of his time. In his mind the natural world consisted of the rocks, the wind, the temperatures, the food supply, partners of the opposite sex and so on. In the competition, for these things some would succeed in passing on their genes to another generation and some would fail. Herbert Spencer coined the phrase "survival of the fittest" for this and Darwin welcomed it. The difference between these two aspects of Darwin's work, the basic theory and the mechanisms involved, is extremely important. It is necessary to keep it clearly in mind because new understandings are emerging from time to time about the factors that cause the changes.

Consider for a moment just the physical environment. The changes that occur over billions of years of Earth's history are enormous. About every 250 million years, for example, all the continents of the world come together into a single contiguous land then subsequently separate into different continents. After another quarter billion years they come together again into a single big continent. There are huge convulsions in these transitions and they transform food supplies. Large ranges of temperature are experienced, and physical conditions generally go through all the variations found anywhere on the surface of the earth. Thus, even in its simplest sense of the physical environment, natural selection carries far more meaning that Darwin could possibly have envisaged in his lifetime. Furthermore, disasters occur today as they have throughout history. Earthquakes, fires, and floods have such an enormous destructive effect on a population that the people who are not killed are the ones that survive. They create the next generation of organisms, not by means of Darwin's natural selection but by sheer luck. In the case of hominids, mating among close relatives was common in earlier times and this caused infertility. They were unable to produce offspring no matter how physically fit they might have been. These are two of the alternatives now available that help explain why species change to new ones over time.

Darwin's ideas concerning mechanisms were influenced by the writings of Thomas Malthus, England's first academic economist, who wrote in 1798 that natural resources are inadequate to provide for a growing population. Malthus observed that plants and animals produce far more offspring than can survive. Humans too, he concluded, can overproduce if left unchecked. The result, in his view, is poverty and starvation, inevitable natural outcomes of population growth. He added that such natural outcomes are God's design to keep humans from getting lazy. It is easy to laugh at these ideas today in light of the modern ability to modify the genetic structure of plants and thereby greatly increase food production. Malthus' reasoning ran like this: increases in food supplies happen by adding new areas of land, so the available amount of food can be doubled in a few years by doubling the total amount of available land. In contrast, a family of eight grown children—a common number and the actual number in Malthus' own family—would increase 50 times as much in the same time period. In mathematical terms the argument runs like this: food production increases arithmetically while populations expand geometrically.

Darwin, who was well acquainted with farm life, recognized the nature of the struggle for life that Malthus was describing and he subsequently employed it as the subtitle to his 1859 book: *The Preservation of Favored Races in the Struggle for Life*. In his mind, Malthus had provided an idea that would guide his research as he concluded that favorable variations would tend to be preserved, and unfavorable ones destroyed. Through such a process new species would emerge. Malthus' ideas are no longer tenable and they received a death blow in the years following World War II when new health programs greatly increased the world's total population without significantly reducing food supplies. A reflection of Malthus' thinking occurred in the late 1960s when a group of experts known as the Club of Rome expressed grave concern over depleting natural resources, warning that some of the ones essential to modern life would disappear before the year 2000 unless drastic measures were taken to limit consumption. These concerns aren't the same today because of the techniques being developed for creating and building up brand new resources from their fundamental molecular components.

Before some of the mechanisms involved are examined, it is necessary to clarify further the point made in the introduction to this book regarding the ancestry of particular organisms. It mentioned the popular fallacy that because humans and apes have almost identical genes the former must have come from the latter. If that were true, then a woman must have come from her sister because they have the same genes. This kind of misunderstanding dates back to Darwin's limited grasp of the mechanisms involved, as was illustrated in Figure 3.2 of Chapter Three. This was how Darwin described the evolution of humans: "Man and all other vertebrate animals have been constructed on the same general model, they pass through the same early stages of development, and they retain certain rudiments in common. Consequently we ought frankly to admit their community of descent. It is only our natural prejudice, and that arrogance which made out forefathers declare that they were descended from demi-gods, which leads us to demur to this conclusion."

Today, people can usually trace their ancestry back two or more generations. In the long history of life, the story may be very different. It is full of surprises as Figure 4.1 illustrates. This figure illustrates the science of cladistics, a field of investigation that finds out how closely related organisms are to one another by the number of characters, of any kind, that they share. The goldfish, cat and human share a common ancestor because all three possess the key feature of a skeletal column. This feature by itself does not tell us if we are more closely related to cats as compared to goldfish. Many common additional traits would need to be included to do that. An examination of these features suggests that the common ancestor of cats and humans lived about 60 million years ago while the common ancestor of goldfish and humans lived about 500 million years ago. Scientists are constantly working at expanding the

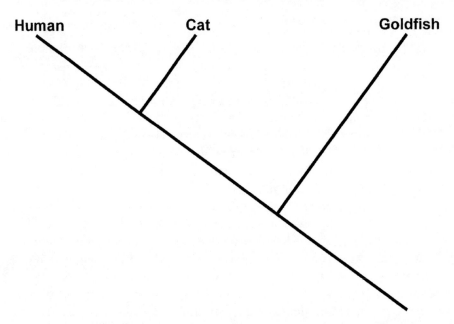

Figure 4.1. This cladogram shows some unexpected linkages in life sequences. The common ancestor of cats and humans lived about 60 million years ago and the common ancestor of goldfish and humans lived about 500 million years ago. Based on S. Conway Morris' *The Crucible of Creation*.

knowledge of these historical lines and they still have a long way to go.

In terms of the mechanisms that operated throughout the billions of years of earth's history, there are several that should be examined. They will provide evidence of the factors that Darwin hinted at, even as he expressed his personal conviction that the main causal factor was natural selection. Furthermore the work is so much easier today with our knowledge of things that were unknown in 1859: DNA, gene research, and the genome project. Darwin's efforts were not sharply focused on the mechanics of change. All his energies were concentrated on refining his basic theory, the seamless thread of life that ran from bacteria to humans. The task of finding the mechanisms was thus left to his successors. Basically, there are two uncertainties about the past: the pace or rate of change, and the direction of what life form followed what. Mutations, then genetic drift and morphology, and finally the views of three leaders—Stephen Jay Gould, Richard Dawkins, and Simon Conway Morris—will be examined next.

Mutations

Changes in the genes of a chromosome can create new traits in the next generation and these changes are unpredictable and frequent. These alterations, or mutations, in existing genes can be as small as a point mutation or as large as a major modification to a chromosome. While they occur in any part of the body, it is their occurrence in the sex cells that is important because these cells determine the form of the next generation of organisms. The frequency of mutations in the sex cells of humans has been calculated at one per tens of thousands for any one gene. Since humans have approximately 32,000 genes, it is to be expected that most sex cells contain at least one gene mutation of some sort. In other words, mutations are probably common occurrences even in healthy people. Most of them are relatively neutral in their effect. They can occur naturally as a result of occasional errors in DNA replication during cell division. They can also happen as a result of exposure to radiation or mercury, and viruses and toxic elements may also be responsible for them.

Genetic Drift

The accidental scattering of genes due to genetic drift is a very big factor in the choice of the organisms that survive and those that become extinct. It is sometimes referred to as "bottle necks" when small populations are isolated or experience a major disaster and what is left becomes a very distorted sampling of the original population. Thus the population that survives and continues to the next stage of development is not representative of the original group. So in the comparison of the various mechanisms that are possible, luck may be as big a factor as anything in how one series of organisms survive and others get destroyed. Sometimes the critical factor is an accident in the lives of humans. At other times it may be due to over-hunting by humans, for example species such as seals or birds.

Another example of genetic drift is known as the founder effect. In this case a small group breaks off from a larger population and forms a new population. The founder effect is probably responsible for the virtually complete lack of blood group B in American Indians, whose ancestors arrived in very small numbers across the Bering Strait during the end of the last Ice Age, about 10,000 years ago. More recent examples are seen in religious isolates like the Dunkers and Old Order Amish of North America. These sects were founded by small numbers of migrants from their much larger congregations in central Europe. They have since remained nearly completely closed to immigration from the surrounding American population. As a result, their blood group gene frequencies are quite different from those in the surrounding populations, both in Europe and in North America.

Morphology

Science recognizes that part of the history of life means a transition from one species to another, and indeed there are fossils representing intermediate stages between one species and another to indicate the transition that has occurred. On the whole, however, the numbers of these transitional forms of life between species are far fewer than one would expect in the normal course of things if the transitions are occurring by a huge number of very small steps. What is found in practice is consistency in the form of different organisms, as if there was some natural series of constraints, like weight and movement and gravity. It seems that only the life forms that take account of these forces of nature survive. There are only a certain number of techniques of swimming that would be appropriate for aquatic animals, whether they be beetles, or snakes or turtles, and similarly, there's a limit to the ways in which our bodies can be structured in order to cope with conditions on the surface on the earth.

This notion of the frequency with which new forms of life have a great deal in common, rather than a multitude of intermediate forms, clashes with the idea of chance as being the successful mechanism. Take swimming as an example. Any organism needs a certain body shape and appendages to be able to swim quickly and to move up, down, and sideways in the water. So we find that fish, reptiles and mammals all have similar body forms for living in water habitats. Fish have fins, seals and whales have flippers and flukes, penguins have paddles and even sea snakes have bodies that are partly flattened. In totally unrelated evolutionary lines and in locations distantly related to one another, similar responses to similar environments are found. These aspects of morphology, which means the study of the shapes or forms of organisms, will be examined more fully later in the chapter when the subject of convergence covered.

Stephen Jay Gould

This is the person who has most strongly advocated the mechanism of natural selection. The theory that nature is entirely arbitrary is the thesis that lies behind that support and Gould has consistently supported it. There is, of course, no way by which you can prove Gould to be right or wrong, but certainly, the fossil record does suggest that this is not exactly the way that things happen over time, and increasingly, more and more questions are being raised about the processes of change in organisms over time.

91

In his political life Gould was part of what might be called the left. He was active in the anti–Vietnam War movement and he identified himself as a Marxist. By insisting on his adherence to this viewpoint, he took the opportunity offered by the popularity of his writings to popularize the validity of a Marxist analysis. At the same time he saw the distortions caused by social Darwinism and at times was caught in it.

While in New York as young man on one occasion, he stayed at a house that was located on a site that had once been the scene of the terrible Triangle Shirtwaist Fire of 1911. In that tragedy, over a hundred textile workers were killed when fire broke out on the eighth floor of the Asch Building in Washington Square, Lower Manhattan. That part of New York had been full of textile sweatshops that were deathtraps because little protection against fire was in place. Gould pointed out that his Jewish immigrant grandparents worked there in that industry.

The history of New York's clothing industry is full of examples of poor working conditions and inadequate safety precautions. The events of March 25, 1911, were exceptional because of the large number of workers killed but other aspects were typical of the times. For instance, it was common practice for management to lock the emergency doors during working hours as was tragically done in the Triangle Shirtwaist factory. This was to prevent workers from stealing things and leaving the building via fire exits instead of the main doors. A shirtwaist, or lady's blouse, was a popular item in the early 1900s and was worth a significant amount of money, the sort of thing that workers might be tempted to steal. There were thousands of these clothing factories in lower Manhattan in the early years of the twentieth century. They employed immigrants, mostly Jewish and Italian, who streamed into New York and found work in the garment industry. Factory managers were able to take advantage of these new arrivals. They had to work 15-hour days to make enough money. Even after 15 hours of work, many of them had to take clothing home to finish in order to complete the quotas that were allocated to them. No health or insurance benefits were provided, no extra money was paid for working overtime, and frequently children were employed. "Sweatshops," and "fire and death traps," were among the terms often used to describe these places of work.

It was in these factories that some of the strongest trade unions took shape to fight for better working conditions. They had to work hard for the right to present workers' grievances to managers. In many cases, the managers refused to recognize their existence and even threatened workers who supported them. In 1909, facing persistent refusal from management to listen to their complaints, 20,000 shirtwaist workers, mainly women—went on strike. There were no laws guaranteeing them this right so business leaders persuaded the police to arrest them for lawless behavior. There were also acts of brutality committed by the police in order to intimidate them. In spite of the conflict, the strike secured some concessions. There was a general pay raise and the work week was fixed at a maximum of 52 hours. The Asch Building at the south of Manhattan Island in New York City was a modern structure and had a reputation for being fireproof. It had 10 floors and the top three were occupied by the Triangle Shirtwaist factory which employed 500. Shortly before five o'clock in the afternoon, as workers were about to leave for the day, a fire broke out on the eighth floor. Like the two other floors above it, there were sewing machines crammed so close together that little aisle space was left for moving about. Scraps of cloth and paper patterns lay around and they quickly contributed to the spread of flames and smoke. The fire had started quickly and flared out just as rapidly. A number of workers from the eighth floor rushed to the stairway in time to see the whole floor erupt in a mass of flames. Many of them managed to escape with their clothes on fire.

It was a different story on the ninth floor. The elevator quit and never reached that floor. The emergency door leading to the fire escape had been locked previously, and by the time someone broke it down, the fire escape had collapsed under the heat of the fire. A few who reached the fire escape were killed as it collapsed. Others, desperate and with nowhere to turn, chose to jump to their death rather than be incinerated. Firemen had difficulty bringing their ladder into position because of the bodies strewed over the pavement, not all of them yet dead. Furthermore, their ladder could only reach as far as the eighth floor. Life nets were brought in to try and catch those falling down but the girls came down with such force that they went right through the nets. It was all over in two hours and firemen were left with the task of removing the bodies of those who had died on one of the upper floors. Altogether 147 workers, almost all of them young women, lost their lives. By the standards of the time the Triangle Shirtwaist Company was not held responsible for the fire and loss of life even though it was quite obvious that it had failed to ensure safety for its workers. Action was taken immediately by city authorities to institute factory inspections, fireproofing, and installation of sprinkler systems. The Union representing the garment workers was not satisfied with these moves. They felt they could no longer trust anyone but themselves for their safety. They took action within a few days of the tragedy.

Parents and friends of the victims of the Triangle fire met with the Ladies' Waist and Dress Makers' Union a few days after the tragedy to give them support. They were completely in favor of the union's demand that the company owners be brought to trial. They were also concerned, as was the union, about the disposal of the $100,000 that had been collected for the families of the victims. These two things galvanized the union. They were convinced that appeals to authorities for corrective action was simply not working and they resolved to be more militant in the future. This is what their president said at the time: "Just because a safety committee was appointed and newspapers devoted pages to the problems in the factories, we cannot assume that the 30,000 shops in the city will suddenly become perfect. As long as the enforcement of labor laws is in the hands of politicians, factories will remain unsafe and unhealthy. We must depend entirely upon ourselves for improvements." In later years other trade unions referred back to them as pioneers of the trade union movement.

Gould observed at the time of his stay in the old shirtwaist factory that it was the corruption of Darwin's ideas that had led directly to the shirtwaist fire. In the early twentieth century, social Darwinists led by Herbert Spencer (who invented the term **survival of the fittest**) began to twist the theory of natural selection to justify all sorts of inequalities, including sweatshop labor in death-trap buildings. Anything that ensured survival of the fittest—that is to say the richest—was justified, it was argued. Darwin's theory about organisms had become a theory about human history. It was one that was picked up by the Russian communists and brutally enforced throughout its 70 years of power. Gould was sympathetic to the ideas of Marx but he disapproved of the way it was applied in the old Soviet Union. Yet he continued to support the thinking of Marx and Engels, the laws of dialectical debate, and he saw how they fitted into the Soviet outlook. There, it was argued, if the workers are sufficiently oppressed there comes a point when they revolt for better conditions. From this style of thinking Gould developed his own variation of evolutionary mechanisms which he called **punctuational change**, prolonged phases of no action with occasional bursts of new life. He felt that this theory fitted biological and geological change better than any of the alternative theories.

Richard Dawkins

This well-known biologist from Oxford University, England, takes a rather extreme view of natural selection and his theory of the mechanism that causes organic change. His book, *The Selfish Gene*, illustrates his neo–Darwinian outlook. That does not mean something different from traditional Darwinism. Dawkins is not only loyal to Darwin's basic theory of evolution, he is equally loyal to Darwin's mechanism of natural selection. He spells it out in *The Selfish Gene* and *The Blind Watchmaker*. Dawkins describes genes as in constant competition, struggling among themselves to see that faithful copies will be represented in the next and in succeeding generations. He takes an extreme view of natural selection, namely that the genes, operating in a purely random manner, determine everything. In one sense this is true, but it fails to take account of the extraordinary things that happen in nature and in populations of organisms. Destructions of large populations occur through natural disasters or human tragedies and in such circumstances it makes no difference what genes are present. Dawkin's theory works quite well on a small scale and, of course, it is perfectly true that in moving from one species to a new one the genes are the critical factors.

95

What the Dawkins theory does not provide for is the many ways in which the total population of genes can be enormously disrupted, and therefore, in the long history of life, this particular theory as a mechanism is quite inadequate. To such criticisms Dawkins insists that he is only pointing out the indispensability of genes in all aspects of the evolutionary process.

Dawkins uses Darwin's idea of small mutational variation to demonstrate that it and it alone is competent to explain the enormous diversity of living things in all their extremes of complexity. He selects the eye to show how natural selection can generate one complex organ, then goes on to conclude that, given vast amounts of time, the complexity of life today arose by the same process of natural selection out of original simplicity. Each successive change in the gradual evolutionary process was simple enough, relative to its predecessor, to have arisen by chance, but the final result is non-random. It is concluded by the survival of the fittest. In fairness to Dawkins, despite the inadequacy of his theory to explain the evolutionary process, there are occasions when spectacular outcomes depend almost entirely on the gene. Dawkins example of the eye fits here. There is a master-control gene, Pax-6, which plays a key role in the formation of eyes. It is a very ancient gene, maybe as old as 600 million years, so it predates the earliest animals. Its function is to produce a light-sensitive unit, something well known in a number of primitive single-celled organisms. So while the role of the gene is vital in cases like the eye, Dawkins's claims for it on the whole are exaggerated because it fails to explain the vast contrasts in morphology and behavior of organisms that have identical genes.

Simon Conway Morris

This professor of evolutionary paleobiology from Cambridge University, England, takes a different view of evolutionary mechanisms compared with the previous two scientists. It's a view that involves a comparison with human life today and is therefore particularly relevant to human evolution, by far the main interest of creationists. The human brain has the outer part, sometimes referred to as the cerebral cortex, wrinkled into a whole series of

Figure 4.2. Ancestors of *Homo sapiens* showed remarkable ability to record their experiences. This 27,000-year-old drawing was discovered on the wall of a cave in France.

folds, as distinct from the inner part of the brain. If you were to spread it out on a flat surface, it would amount to an area of three feet by three feet, but in its present form it is all packed together tightly. The question is how does this fit with the idea of a very gradual series of changes over long periods of time, the mechanism of chance that both Gould and Dawkins propose? The answer is not known. It is known that the hominid predecessors of **Homo sapiens** doubled their brain size in the evolutionary short time span of two million years. It is also known that hominids from 27,000 years ago could record aspects of their history. Morris has some quite new ideas about evolutionary mechanisms that might explain how brain size can change so much in two million years. His ideas begin with present day events.

Evolution and Creationism in the Public Schools

Whenever humankind wants to investigate something that happened in the past, it calls for a look at all the possible documents or artifacts or information of any kind that can help reconstruct what took place. Having completed that piece of research, which corresponds in evolution to finding all the possible fossils, then the existing situation today is examined, just as people would in any investigation of human problems. Since humans are part of this whole story of evolution, the way that they behave in regard to investigating a matter in their own sphere of activity and interest may well be similar to the way that other forms of life behave. The approach of Simon Morris is to examine the history of life in the same way one would examine a problem in human history. People never think of their individual lives, their family lives, their community and national lives as being random, totally without cause or consequence for themselves or others. Everyday decisions are made by them and by others that affect them, and they have to adjust to cope with the changes. Why do people set themselves apart from all other forms of life and think that life is different for them, imagining in the process that other life, unlike humankind, are victims of their environments? That is the question that Morris asks and for which he proposes an answer.

Think of the ways that one organism interacts with another in today's human society, then take that idea back into the history of life and apply it to the relationships between organisms at different times along the billions of years of earth's history. Look at the ways human societies organize their lives once they emerge from what might be called jungle existence. Rules for behavior are established, property rights get recognized, ethical codes emerge, and there are consequences if people violate their community norms. These are things that can be found anywhere in the world, not only today when it is so easy to imitate others but in past times when there were societies largely isolated from one another. These patterns of life were similar all over the world and, with the passage of time, they were enriched by cross-cultural interactions and by imitating other communities. Cannot other than human forms of life do likewise? Can they not learn by imitation, or from observing how others cope with predators or sudden changes in environments, and so survive?

The word that defines the Morris approach to evolutionary mechanisms is **convergence**, the tendency of organisms to develop similar forms and abilities over time. He says that all the evidence to date supports this. The forms that emerge in the history of time tend to become similar in different parts of the world, quite independently of one another. So, as one would expect from human history today, there may well be activity among organisms as they interact with one another, influencing the forms that emerge. And so, in Morris's view, there is a convergence that could be expected to express itself today, after say 500 million years, in lives that look like humans. There is no reason to expect precisely what did happen, given the reality of chance factors over time, but there is a good reason in Morris' view to expect life forms similar to humans at the end of 500 million years of evolutionary history. This view is in sharp contrast to the two just considered, those of Gould and Dawkins. In their minds, everything is unpredictable because chance rules at all times. Over 500 million years, as they see it, anything might happen. Science fiction writers pick up on this view and write accordingly.

Evolution then, according to the Morris view, is not governed by chance but must operate within certain constraints. Just as humans learn by solving problems, so earlier forms of life learned to solve problems in similar ways. There is a limited number of solutions to the problems which organisms encounter in the natural environment. Their solutions to problems are not always predictable, but the probabilities of outcomes can be gauged. Consider, for example, what's now known from the massive research of the 1990s about the human brain. Much of its modes of operation, as has been discovered, have changed little in thousands of years, so that reactions to present day events may be identical to those of thousands of years ago even though the circumstances are totally different. Take as an example the role of fear in human experience. Scientists know from research and from direct observation of brain activity in real time that fear triggers flows of chemicals away from normal brain operations into strengthening of muscles and accelerating blood clotting. The reason for this is that the brain activates survival procedures before a person decides what to do because its memory does not differentiate between a lion attack and an angry face. It is the same brain structure that human ancestors had in the jungle thousands of years ago.

What is known from recent brain research about the best way to learn? It is always the same, problem solving. When humans are confronted with relevant and manageable problems, the brain is structured from long-standing experience to find solutions. If the problem is relevant, which is the same as saying that it vitally affects the life of the person, then one would expect that the brain would work best when attempting to find a solution. It could be a life or death type of problem. In the Europe of 15,000 years ago, it might have been how to get out of the cave to find food without disturbing the bears. The brains that tackled the problem at that time were structured just like the ones we have today, with similar genes and similar survival mechanisms deeply embedded in billion of cells. Nowadays, in universities and schools at all levels, problem-solving approaches have become the normal method of instruction. The good results already observed are solid evidence of its value and the results of research on earlier life forms tell us that other species discovered this mode of learning long before there was a *Homo sapiens*.

Convergent evolution means that different kinds of unrelated organisms solve their problems in the same ways. For example, bats and dolphins use echolocation to locate prey. To say this, as Morris does, carries no suggestion of a planner, or creator, being involved. Nevertheless, those who do not agree with his conclusions imply that he has moved away from true science into the realm of speculation or even religion. As we will see later, Morris bases his views on specific research findings and completely rejects the idea that his views are based on anything outside the scientific field. It is very important, in the ongoing conflict between scientists and creationists, that scientists avoid data that are nonscientific. The United States National Association of Biology Teachers recently discovered how easy it is to step outside its field of competence and make unwarranted claims. It had defined its position regarding evolution in this way, "The diversity of life on earth is the outcome of evolution: an unsupervised, impersonal, unpredictable, and natural process." Someone challenged the use of the words unsupervised and impersonal as going beyond scientific knowledge. Fortunately, the association agreed and eliminated the two words. Excesses of scientists are just as harmful to good science as are the extravagant claims of creationists.

Scientists from as far back as the middle of the nineteenth century have been aware of convergent evolution and frequently described examples of it with fascination and joy. The architectural parallelism of the wings of a bat or bird which arose independently yet resulted from a similar modification of the vertebrate forelimb was one example. The streamlined profile of a shark or fish was another. More recently a quite new aspect of convergence appeared. Researchers began to look for it among molecules. They had already found striking analogies between the antifreeze proteins that allowed two unrelated groups of fish swimming on opposite ends of the globe to survive in icy waters. They also detected a bizarre form of antibody protein in species as different as camels and sharks. Rudolf A. Raff, an evolutionary developmental biologist at the Molecular Biology Institute of Indiana University, expressed great interest in this aspect of his work. He sees it as a valuable part of the mechanisms of evolution. His view is quite similar to that of Morris. He sees convergence happening because organisms keep wanting to

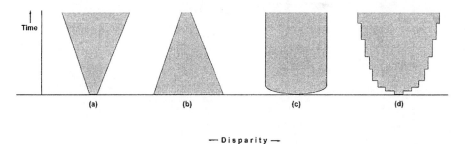

— Disparity —

Figure 4.3. Here are different views of the history of life over the last 500 million years. Diagram (b) was the one advocated by Stephen Jay Gould, that of decreasing disparity with time. Diagram (d) was the position held by Simon Conway Morris, that of increasing disparity with time but at varying rates. Based on S. Conway Morris' *The Crucible of Creation.*

do similar things and environmental limits determine that there are only so many ways of doing them.

Morris, who is an expert on the Burgess Shale, a five-hundred-million-year-old rich deposit of fossils in eastern British Columbia, Canada, summarizes his convictions about convergence in the following way. Imagine that humans were living half a billion years ago, trying to predict what the history of life might look like in the

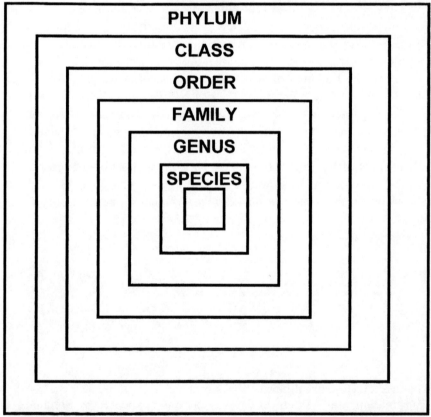

KINGDOM

PHYLUM

CLASS

ORDER

FAMILY

GENUS

SPECIES

Figure 4.4. This is the traditional hierarchal classification of the seven major groups of organisms, first used by the Linnean Society of London.

future. Would their vision resemble any one of the drawings in Figure 4.3? The (a) drawing represents the traditional view, that disparity steadily increased through geological time, (b) maximum disparity existed at the time of the Cambrian, then decreased with time, (c) disparity increased rapidly in the Cambrian and stayed the same subsequently, and (d) disparity increased rapidly in the Cambrian and increased at varying rates since that time. Keep in mind that disparity means the number of animals with different anatomy and shape, while diversity means the total number of different kinds of animals.

Morris concludes that Gould and Dawkins would choose (b) because they think that chance determines everything. While there was obviously a large disparity during the Cambrian period, most of the types and their descendants would become extinct over time in the fight for survival and the world would be left with fewer types at the present time. In the mind of Conway Morris, (d) is a better

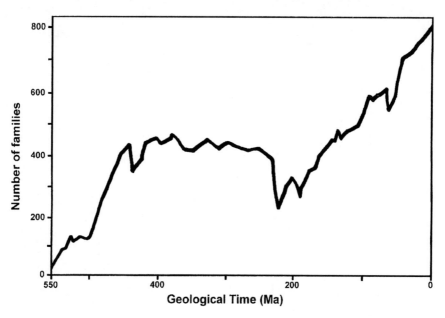

Figure 4.5. This chart shows the increase in diversity of marine mammals since Cambrian times. Based on S. Conway Morris' "The Crucible of Creation."

fit because innovations take place in the long history of evolution and these lead to new forms of life, providing many varieties of anatomy and shape. He supported this view with reference to the extensive research that had been conducted on trilobites as one example from many research reports. Trilobites were multicelled animals with a nervous system and muscles that became extinct about 250 million years ago. They left large numbers of fossils and the research report that Morris quoted showed a fascinating sequence of developments extending over a hundred million years. A large number of body plans was identified, each slightly larger and a little different in shape over this period of time, and each better suited than its immediate predecessor to cope within its given environment.

FIVE

Genesis and Science

Creation scientists, in all the different ways in which they express their beliefs in an intelligent designer who created the universe, invariably base some of their claims on the early chapters of the book of Genesis. They are convinced that the earth as humankind knows it today was created at one time in the past, not something that evolved over time. A large number of them see these early chapters of Genesis as real history in which the creation of all things occurred in six days of 24 hours each. Adam and Eve are often described as the first man and woman on earth. Their disobedience, according to these creationists, coupled with Noah's worldwide flood, destroyed most forms of life on earth and greatly affected the natural order. Most creation scientists believe that the earth is thousands rather than billions of years old.

Because of this close association with Genesis on the part of creationists, it is here, in these beginning chapters of the Bible, that the evolution and creationism conflict needs to be carefully analyzed. The dividing lines between a scientist's study of the natural world and the approaches taken by others are vividly portrayed in these chapters. They provide excellent content for demonstrating the distinctiveness of the scientific mode of inquiry. In addition, the setting provides an occasion to investigate the scientific validity or otherwise of the content of this ancient literature. This study will begin with the first two chapters of Genesis, taken from a modern translation of the English Bible. After examining these, chapter seven of Genesis will be looked at next. It is on the value reeationists see in these three chapters that most creationists claims rest.

Genesis Chapters One and Two

In the beginning when God created the heavens and the earth, the earth was a formless void and darkness covered the face of the deep, while a wind from God swept over the face of the waters. Then God said, "Let there be light"; and there was light. And God saw that the light was good; and God separated the light from the darkness. God called the light Day, and the darkness he called Night. And there was evening and there was morning, the first day. And God said, "Let there be a dome in the midst of the waters, and let it separate the waters from the waters." So God made the dome and separated the waters that were under the dome from the waters that were above the dome. And it was so. God called the dome Sky. And there was evening and there was morning, the second day.

And God said, "Let the waters under the sky be gathered together into one place, and let the dry land appear." And it was so. God called the dry land Earth, and the waters that were gathered together he called Seas. And God saw that it was good. Then God said, "Let the earth put forth vegetation: plants yielding seed and fruit trees of every kind on earth that bear fruit with the seed in it." And it was so. The earth brought forth vegetation: plants yielding seed of every kind, and trees of every kind bearing fruit with the seed in it. And God saw that it was good. And there was evening and there was morning, the third day. And God said, "Let there be lights in the dome of the sky to separate the day from the night; and let them be for signs and for seasons and for days and years, and let them be lights in the dome of the sky to give light upon the earth." And it was so. God made the two great lights—the greater light to rule day and the lesser light to rule the night—and the stars. God set them in the dome of the sky to give light upon the earth, to rule over the day and over the night, and to separate the light from the darkness. And God saw that it was good. And there was evening and there was morning, the fourth day.

And God said, "Let the waters bring forth swarms of living creatures, and let birds fly above the earth across the dome of the sky." So God created the great sea monsters, and every living creature that moves, of every kind, with which the waters

106

swarm, and every winged bird of every kind. And God saw that it was good. God blessed them, saying, "Be fruitful and multiply and fill the waters in the seas, and let the birds multiply on the earth." And there was evening and there was morning, the fifth day. And God said, "Let the earth bring forth living creatures of every kind: cattle and creeping things and wild animals of the earth of every kind." And it was so. God made the wild animals of the earth of every kind, and the cattle of every kind, and everything that creeps upon the ground of every kind. And God saw that it was good.

Then God said, "Let us make humankind in our image, according to our likeness; and let them have dominion over the fish of the sea, and over the birds of the air, and over the cattle, and over all the wild animals of the earth, and over every creeping thing that creeps upon the earth." So God created humankind in his image, in the image of God he created them; male and female he created them. God blessed them, and God said to them, "Be fruitful and multiply, and fill the earth and subdue it; and have dominion over the fish of the sea and over the birds of the air and over every living thing that moves upon the earth." God said, "See, I have given you every plant yielding seed that is upon the face of all the earth, and every tree with seed in its fruit; you shall have them for food. And to every beast of the earth, and to every bird of the air, and to everything that creeps on the earth, everything that has the breath of life, I have given every green plant for food." And it was so. God saw everything that he had made, and indeed, it was very good. And there was evening and there was morning, the sixth day.

Thus the heavens and the earth were finished, and all their multitude. And on the seventh day God finished the work that he had done, and he rested on the seventh day from all the work that he had done. So God blessed the seventh day and hallowed it, because on it God rested from all the work that he had done in creation. These are the generations of the heavens and the earth when they were created. In the day that the Lord God made the earth and the heavens, when no plant of the field was yet in the earth and no herb of the field had yet sprung up—for the Lord God had not caused it to rain upon the earth, and there was no one to till the ground; but a stream would rise from the earth, and water the whole face of the ground—then the Lord God formed man from the dust of the ground, and breathed into his nostrils the breath of life; and the man became a living being. And the Lord God planted a garden in Eden, in the east; and there he put the man whom he had formed. Out of the ground the Lord God made to grow every tree that is pleasant to the sight and good for food, the tree of life also in the midst of the garden, and the tree of the knowledge of good and evil.

A river flows out of Eden to water the garden, and from there it divides and becomes four branches. The name of the first is Pishon: it is the one that flows around the whole land of Havilah, where there is gold; and the gold of that land is good; bdellium and onyx stone are there. The name of the second river is Gihon; it is the one that flows around the whole land of Cush. The name of the third river is Tigris, which flows east of Assyria. And the fourth river is the Euphrates. The Lord God took the man and put him in the garden of Eden to till it and keep it. And the Lord God commanded the man, "You may eat of every tree of the garden; but of the tree of the knowledge of good and evil you shall not eat, for in the day that you eat of it you shall die."

Then the Lord God said, "It is not good that the man should be alone; I will make him a helper as his partner." So out of the ground the Lord God formed every animal of the field and every bird of the air, and brought them to the man to see what he would call them; and whatever the man called every living creature, that was its name. The man gave names to all cattle, and to the birds of the air, and to every animal of the field; but for the man, there was not found a helper as his partner. So the Lord God caused a deep sleep to fall upon the man, and he slept; then he took one of his ribs and closed up its place with flesh. And the rib that the Lord God had taken from the man he made into a woman and brought her to the man. Then the man said, "This at last is bone of my bones and flesh of my flesh; this one shall be called Woman, for out of Man this one was taken." Therefore a man leaves his father and his mother and clings to his wife, and they become one flesh. And the man and his wife were both naked, and were not ashamed.

These chapters have been revered throughout history. The fact that they have been preserved for more than two thousand years is an indication of their value. Encyclopedia Britannica summarizes their status in both Christian and Muslim traditions: In the Judeo-Christian and Islamic traditions, Adam and Eve are the parents of the human race. Genesis gives two versions of their creation. In the first, God creates "male and female in his own image" on the sixth day. In the second, Adam is placed in the Garden of Eden, and Eve is later created from his rib to ease his loneliness. For succumbing to temptation and eating the fruit of the forbidden tree of knowledge of good and evil, God banished them from Eden, and they and their descendants were forced to live lives of hardship. Cain and Abel were their children. Christian theologians developed the doctrine of original sin based on the story of their transgression; in contrast, the Quran teaches that Adam's sin was his alone and did not make all people sinners.

Theologians and Biblical scholars have examined the record in Genesis in detail and have published their findings in many thousands of books that occupy space in libraries today. For the most part, the original record was cherished because of its symbolic value. Examples of transcendent wisdom were found there that helped illuminate later parts of the Biblical record. Some churches today, like creationists, see them as historical accounts, just like any other record of past events. It is quite common to find statements in their publications like the following: God created the whole universe in six days of 24 hours each, with humankind appearing at the same time, a new species of life on earth to whom God intended to entrust global government. It is very important to emphasize here that there are different ways of knowing. Scientists investigate the natural world and seek explanations for what they find. It is a limited form of knowledge and every true scientist avoids making claims that go beyond the data at hand. It is entirely proper for both scientists and others to have different kinds of knowledge, each as important and true in its own domains as scientific understandings are in science. Art forms express their understandings in one form while faith in transcendent experiences is demonstrated in another.

Great scientists have always understood this, and their lives and words stress the need for intellectual humility in the face of all that has yet to be known. Isaac Newton beautifully epitomized this in words like the following, in 1827, shortly before his death: "I see myself like a boy playing on the seashore, now and then finding a smoother pebble or a prettier shell, while the great ocean of truth lay all undiscovered before me." The writers who recorded these ancient accounts were gifted people, probably as gifted as any university professor of today, yet limited by the available knowledge of the time in which it was written. Scientific knowledge is always growing. Some things are left behind as new discoveries replace them while others are confirmed and become part of a permanent body of knowledge. How then does a scientist approach an ancient passage of literature like these two chapters of Genesis? How is the approach different from that of theologians or church leaders? The answer is, the scientist will discover data that time and subsequent research have validated, while he or she will ignore the presence of other data that are not of the scientific genre. Examine then, as scientists do, assuming no belief that the Bible is different from any other ancient document, these two chapters from the beginning of Genesis.

The first paragraph of the seven above says that the earth had a beginning in time, and that its condition prior to the action of God was a formless dark void. We know today that the earth did have a beginning in time. In fact geologists are now examining records in stone that date back billions of years close to that starting time. The vast amount of dust particles that preceded the beginning could probably be described as dark and void. The claim for the agency of God is of course beyond scientific knowledge. Creationists can consider it as one of the mechanisms involved, as they do, in the evolution of planet earth, but scientists must be careful to leave that data aside because it is not experimentally verifiable. There is one other thing in that first paragraph that interests scientists because it fits present knowledge. It is the presence of light in the cosmos prior to the appearance of the sun. We know that the cosmos had a beginning in time that predates the earth by eight or nine billion years and in the course of that long period of time innumerable numbers of stars shone their lights across the expanse of space.

Before leaving this first paragraph, it needs to be said that the beauty of language, the flow and cadence of repeated phrases, and the overall simplicity of the narrative are all good reasons for its having been preserved down the ages. The writers must have been competent and clear thinkers. However, as will be seen later in this chapter, the cosmic framework of mind within which they operated was altogether different from today's mind, and this greatly limits the amount of data in their writings that one can link in any way with present scientific knowledge. This will be clear as the second of the above paragraphs is examined because so much of it is in non-scientific language. At the same time there is one thing that comes at the very beginning, water, before there is any mention of life forms, and this would naturally catch the eye of any biologist. Biologists know now that water is always associated with the emergence of life. That is why so much effort is spent investigating the possibility of finding water on Mars. If there is water there, then in all likelihood some form of life will also be there. It was fortuitous, or maybe it was unusual insight, that made the author of Genesis record the presence of water before there was any mention of life forms.

The next two paragraphs deal with the next three days and cover the appearance of the sun, moon, and stars, plus a variety of life forms. The notable exception among the latter are humans and it soon becomes obvious, as it continues, that the focus of the entire two chapters is the story of humanity. All the earlier detail is a backdrop for it. Apart from the mention of water before life is mentioned there is nothing that can be connected from these two paragraphs with present knowledge of life forms and their evolution. Darwin's theory rules supreme. It is well authenticated by the discoveries and work of thousands of scientists. It traces the evolution of all forms of life, including humans, from some simple original forms of life that existed billions of years ago. As was seen in the previous chapter, the mechanisms involved in the evolution of these myriads of living things is still an open question. The facts of their common origin is not. In the original waters of earth the first kind of life was found and via different mechanisms all subsequent life emerged, both the billions that are now extinct and the ones seen today.

111

The remaining four paragraphs are entirely concerned with humans. It is quite clear that the author, or authors as seems more likely, regarded the entire work of creation as having happened in order to provide a suitable environment for humans, one in which this new species would be given a dominant caretaker responsibility. Readers can easily connect the concept of one dominant species with what is known today. The final stage in Darwin's evolutionary process, as one might call it until a better species is known, is *Homo sapiens*, and this species has characteristics that no other possesses. These are not anatomical features because some species that lived more than a million years earlier had almost identical body appearances and similar motor skills to those of ours. The unique feature of *Homo sapiens*, at least in the degree in which it now exists, is human consciousness. It enables humans to understand and keep a record of the past as a species and, from that record, it equips us to predict our future to some extent. Are there any data in all of these paragraphs that connect the narrative with places on the surface of the earth? Yes, clearly in paragraph six, in the references to the rivers Tigris and Euphrates, the area once known as Mesopotamia, now the nation of Iraq.

The creation of the cosmos and its earthly life forms, initially in Mesopotamia, leading to the emergence of humans was the central purpose in the first two chapters. The next five chapters, a litany of death, debauchery, and lawlessness, record what happened to humans after they disobeyed God. By the time one reaches chapter six it seems that God has changed his mind and is about to destroy the entire human race. For creationists, it was their act of disobedience that caused all these bad things, and led in time to the world of disorder with which many are familiar today. No scientist can accept that, because it fails to explain any present day proven facts about humanity. Death and mayhem, much of it much worse than is recorded in chapters three to six, occurred among the humans who lived thousands of years before the book of Genesis was written. There may be other reasons for the destructive record of human failure throughout history. Creationists may choose to build an argument for intelligent design on these early chapters of Genesis, and an argument for human mischief down the centuries on the basis of one act of disobedience, but they should not call it science. It belongs in theology, in the domain of belief.

The other part of Genesis that is repeatedly quoted by creationists to explain earth's history and the disruption that occurred in its physical environment is the story of Noah's Flood. Chapter seven of Genesis gives an account of it. In this case there is a valuable link between Noah's Flood and some scientific research presently being conducted in an area to which reference is made in the Genesis account. In contrast to Genesis one and two, the flood story is much closer to verifiable historical events. Once again, it is necessary to add that this does not make the story of creation fictitious. It is just not based on scientific facts. The following chapter seven will give us the main part of the flood account. I will refer to the previous and following chapters as needed.

Genesis Chapter Seven

Then the Lord said to Noah, "Go into the ark, you and all your household, for I have seen that you alone are righteous before me in this generation. Take with you seven pairs of all clean animals, the male and its mate; and a pair of the animals that are not clean, the male and its mate; and seven pairs of the birds of the air also, male and female, to keep their kind alive on the face of the earth. For in seven days I will send rain on the earth for forty days and forty nights; and every living thing that I have made I will blot out from the face of the ground. And Noah did all that the Lord had commanded him. Noah was six hundred years old when the flood of waters came on the earth. And Noah with his sons and his wife and his sons' wives went into the ark to escape the waters of the flood. Of clean animals, and of animals that are not clean, and of birds, and of everything that creeps on the ground, two and two, male and female, went into the ark with Noah, as God had commanded Noah. And after seven days the waters of the flood came on the earth.

In the six hundredth year of Noah's life, in the second month, on the seventeenth day of the month, on that day all the fountains of the great deep burst forth, and the windows of the heavens were opened. The rain fell on the earth forty days and forty nights. On the very same day Noah with his sons, Shem and Ham and Japheth, and Noah's wife and the three wives of his sons entered the ark, they and every wild animal of every kind, and all domestic animals of every kind, and every creeping thing that creeps on the earth, and every bird of every kind–every bird, every winged creature. They went into the ark with Noah, two and two of all flesh in which there was the breath of life. And those that entered, male and female, of all flesh, went in as God had commanded him; and the Lord shut him in.

The flood continued forty days on the earth; and the waters increased, and bore up the ark, and it rose high above the earth. The waters swelled and increased greatly on the earth; and the ark floated on the face of the waters. The waters swelled so mightily on the earth that all the high mountains under the whole heaven were covered; the waters swelled above the mountains, covering them fifteen cubits deep. And all flesh died that moved on the earth, birds, domestic animals, wild animals, all swarming creatures that swarm on the earth, and all human beings; everything on dry land in whose nostrils was the breath of life died. He blotted out every living thing that was on the face of the ground, human beings and animals and creeping things and birds of the air; they were blotted out from the earth. Only Noah was left, and those that were with him in the ark. And the waters swelled on the earth for one hundred fifty days.

Because the flood story is closer to verifiable historical events than the creation narrative, it is important that we identify the limitations in the Genesis account. For example, when the word kind is employed in Genesis it usually means species. One of the strong arguments among creationists at an earlier point was the inviolability of species. Each one had to be a separate creation of God. Thus, when Noah was instructed to take pairs of animals and so on of each kind, each pair represented a species. In this way, since only within species can there be a guarantee of reproduction, life could be preserved after the flood. There are probably twenty million species of life alive today and this number has not changed significantly for millions of years. Even if we subdivide and subdivide this total number we are left with an impossible task for Noah if he were to preserve all the main types of life on land. Alongside the problem of numbers, the ark—about the same floor area as a large store in a shopping mall—had to accommodate food supplies for a year, prevent mould and pests, and provide the fresh food essential for some animals such as snakes.

As was stated earlier, the understanding of the universe was inadequate at this time. There were ideas about huge quantities of water existing above the dome and other quantities beneath the ground to which reference is made in the second paragraph above, "The fountains of the great deep were broken up." Chapter Two records the work of Thomas Burnet, who was determined to make science and the Bible harmonize. He knew that all the oceans of

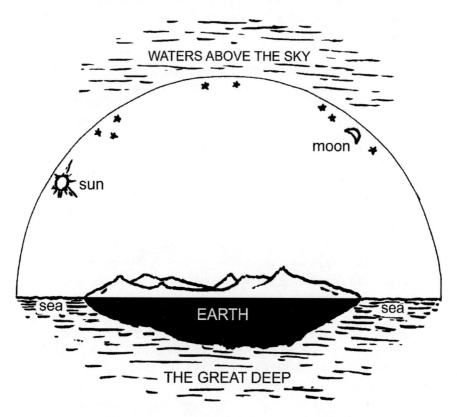

Figure 5.1. This is how the ancient Hebrew viewed the cosmos.

the world would not be sufficient to cover all of global earth, but he was sure that the flood had to cover the whole globe. He invoked the ancient Hebrew idea of stores of water beneath the earth, and he was aided in his attempts to make it fit by his friend Isaac Newton. If we make use of present-day knowledge, we now know that the total quantity of water operating in the hydrologic cycle, the process of evaporation from oceans and subsequent change into rain or snow, is incapable of covering parts of the surface of the earth more than a few feet of depth at any one time. Additionally, some parts of the earth have never known more than a few inches of rain, at least within the last few million years. Whatever the flood was, it could not have been more than a local event.

There are stories about floods all over the world, and these have been picked up by creationists as evidence of a world wide flood, but the stories are all different in type and in scale. There are no traces of any kind of flood in Greenland and Antarctica, for example. Mountain tops show the characteristic age-old sedimentary formations that date back millions of years and there is no evidence of flood damage in tree rings that go back as much as 30,000 years. Perhaps the weakest argument of all lies in the claim that fossil-bearing strata were deposited by the flood waters. Did they include the fossils from those animals that became extinct millions of years ago? As with the creation narratives, all descriptions of Noah's flood must be assessed in terms of what was known of the rest of the world and its physical processes. It may come as a new idea to those who read the Bible literally, treating it as an accurate record of history, that more than one scholar proposed an external source rather than transcendental revelation for the creation and flood accounts in Genesis. One event in 1872 gave rise to this possibility for the first time.

Darwin's *Origin of Species* created an enormous public reaction in Britain when it was first published because it implied that the account of creation in Genesis must be completely wrong. The public outcry led to increased interest in archeological work in the Middle East. Thousands of cuneiform tablets had been unearthed in Iraq over the years and brought to England and the British Museum was anxious to understand them better. These tablets are

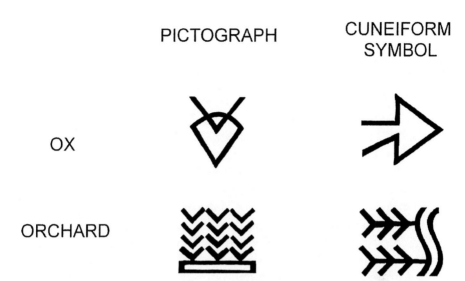

Figure 5.2. The earliest form of writing was pictographic, simple pictures of objects. In later times these pictographs were changed into cuneiform symbols.

blocks of hardened clay that had been inscribed with wedge-shaped patterns while still wet. Once dried they are as hard as cement and can last for thousands of years. In 1872, just 13 years after Darwin's publication, one of these cuneiform tablets that arrived back in London was found to have a detailed description of an ancient flood that closely matched the Biblical account. Its date of origin was the seventh century B.C. The hero who featured in the tablet had built a huge boat to protect people from a flood which was said to cover the world. George Smith was the archeologist who brought the tablet back to the British Museum.

This account of a flood went on to describe how the boat eventually came to rest on a mountain and the hero released a dove which returned to the boat because it could not find a resting place. He sent out a swallow but it also returned. Finally he sent out a raven which never returned so everyone knew then that the waters had receded. George Smith's discovery created so much interest that England's Prime Minister adjourned the nation's Parliament for a day in order to attend Smith's lecture on the tablet. Is it possible that the Biblical account of the flood was a copy of an older record that had been circulating in Mesopotamia, the Gilgamesh legend, and was recorded on cuneiform tablets at the same time as the Jews were there? It is an interesting hypothesis, and one that is worth testing. Smith later returned to Mesopotamia, aided by a special grant of $3,000 from the *Daily Telegraph* newspaper. He discovered additional information on the flood part of the Gilgamish legend such as the following: "The sea grew quiet, the tempest was still, the flood ceased. I looked at the weather, stillness had set in, and all of mankind had returned to play. The landscape was as level as a flat roof. On Mount Nizir, the ship came to a halt. Mount Nizir held the ship fast, allowing no motion."

First reactions to the Gilgamish legend was that it reinforced the biblical story. The portions of the clay tablets that George Smith had brought back to England and presented at the special lecture gave enough of the story to give this impression. However, within days of his return to Mesopotamia, now Iraq, George Smith stumbled on some other portions of the Gilgamish legend, a record of the creation of the world—something that no one had expected him to find. As a result, the search for ancient records and cuneiform tablets was greatly intensified and large numbers of tablets were unearthed, not only in Iraq but in neighboring areas of the surrounding region, and more and more of these tablets extended the descriptions of both creation and flood.

Christopher de Hamel in *The Book: A History of the Bible*, proposed a possible explanation for these accounts of creation and the flood. De Hamel noted in his book that in the year 597 B.C., close to the time when the first of George Smith's cuneiform tablets was written, King Nebuchadnezzar of Babylon had conquered Jerusalem and taken a large number of Jews into captivity in Babylon.

There they stayed for several generations until, after about 70 years when that part of Babylon was conquered by King Cyrus of Persia, the captives were released and allowed to go back to Jerusalem. De Hamel suggests that the records of the early part of Genesis were not even written before the return of the captives to Jerusalem because the Bible itself gives very little information about the existence of sacred scrolls. So much of Jewish history was oral, retained in this form by the priests among the Hebrews rather than written down. He goes on to point out that it was some time after the captives had gone back to Jerusalem at the end of the captivity that Ezra is identified as a scribe in Jerusalem. He had also come back from captivity and was busy explaining the various documents that had been written. It seems fairly certain that the early part of Genesis was finally committed to documentary form at that time. It certainly is evident from the Bible that from the time of the return from captivity, there is clearly an authentic written text that covers the early part of Genesis as well as the rest of that part of the Old Testament. All of this history casts quite a new light on the Bible— the whole origin of the record is cast in a much wider cultural setting than is generally assumed.

Black Sea and the Last Ice Age

Two events that were separated in time by thousands of years came together in the 1990s as a result of extensive oceanographic research on the Mediterranean and the Black Sea. The findings from that scientific work revolutionized our understanding of the Black Sea and they also helped to clear away false legendary stories about Noah's flood. Here is a look at some of the details of these findings and how new insights into the Black Sea's changing environment affected the lives of the hunters and gatherers who lived on its shores thousands of years ago. The Black Sea is close to Mesopotamia, or Iraq, the setting for the creation accounts as well as the narrative about Noah's Flood. The first research study focused on the final phases of the last ice age which began about a million years ago. In that period of time, there was a build up of massive ice sheets on land because of a sustained drop in the world's average temperature. Throughout the million years, conditions waxed and waned in response to fluctuations in temperature but, for large stretches of time (sometimes as long as 50,000 years), the ice sheets built up to depths of more than a mile.

All of northern North America and Europe was covered with these huge ice sheets. Water was withdrawn from the ocean as pre-

119

cipitation built up the mass of ice on land, lowering the level of the sea all around the world by as much as 300 feet. Some idea of the extent to which the water of the ocean was withdrawn can be gleaned from measurements at the east coast of the United States where, at the height of the accumulation of ice, the shore was 200 miles further out into the Atlantic than it is today. In addition to the withdrawal of water, the land was pressed down under the weight of the ice, creating a bowl-shaped depression over large areas. The southern edges of the ice sheets, where temperatures were just above the freezing point, were dotted with heaps of gravel and rocks that were released by the ice as it melted. These outwash moraines as they were called interfered with the free flow of the meltwaters and consequently groups of lakes formed along the southern edges of the ice. The Great Lakes between Canada and the U.S. first took shape in this way.

About 14,000 years ago, the first of the major melt phases of the Europe and Asia ice sheet began. Large lakes began to form on the southern margins as the ice retreated northward and more and more debris collected behind it. Some water escaped toward the south into the Black Sea but most remained trapped at the southern edge of the ice sheets. A second and much faster rate of melting developed between 7,000 and 8,000 years ago. As the ice retreated still farther northward, the terminal moraines cut off all flow of water to the south and all meltwater was directed into the North Sea. These meltwater phases involved huge quantities of water and their destructive effects on many places gave rise to numerous accounts of floods all over the northern hemisphere. The disruption of historic water channels was one of the more permanent effects of the meltwater cycles. Streams that for thousands of years had fed lakes suddenly changed their courses and ran in the opposite direction. The Black Sea was one lake that lost its traditional supply of fresh water from its northern rivers as the terminal moraines redirected water toward the North Sea. Its level dropped. At the same time ocean levels were rising as the ice sheets melted. By about 7,000 years ago, the Black Sea was 300 feet lower in elevation that its nearest ocean, the Mediterranean. At that time the eastern part of the Bosporus was a land bridge that shut off the Black Sea from the Mediterranean.

The Black Sea Flood

The transition at the eastern end of the Bosporus from a land bridge to a waterway is the second research study that we will now examine. It's a study that began in the 1950s as the U.S., concerned about the behavior and locations of Soviet submarines, launched a worldwide series of investigations of the ocean's floors. The Cold War was at a point of high tension at these times. As so often happens in the history of science, researchers begin work on a project for a particular purpose and then discover, almost by accident as it were, even greater things. This happened with the second research study and it is included here as an illustration of good scientific work. As the ocean's depths were being measured mile after mile, a continuous undersea midocean mountain chain was discovered, running all around the earth. From its center, volcanic rock was con-

Figure 5.3. The modern day version of Noah's Flood holds that post-glacial meltwaters in the Mediterranean Sea burst through the old Bosporus land bridge and flooded both the Black Sea and much of Mesopotamia.

stantly erupting and spreading in opposite directions toward the continents. The large oceanic tectonic plates had been discovered and the secrets of mountain building and much of the world's volcanic actions were at last understood. To continue the examination of ocean floor research, the Mediterranean and Black seas came under scrutiny by the 1960s. The Woods Hole Oceanographic Institute was commissioned by the U.S. Government to examine the Bosporus and Black Sea areas. It was a difficult mission. The U.S. had just given Turkey nuclear-armed bombers and so the Soviet Union was particularly suspicious of any U.S. activity as close to its shores as the Black Sea.

The Woods Hole research vessel began a zigzag course from the western Mediterranean through the Bosporus into the Black Sea, under the watchful eyes of Soviet warships and aircraft. About halfway through, two discoveries were made at a point where the channel was only half a mile wide. Unique noises from the ship's depth sounder indicated that a channel had been cut in solid rock some time in the past. It was a very deep cut and indicated that enormous force must have once been exercised on that part of the channel. The other discovery was the existence of two flows of water in the channel, a deep saltwater one flowing eastward and a freshwater surface one flowing westward. Conversations with local people confirmed that this double waterway had always been there. Fishers were known to make use of it by lowering a basket of stones down into the eastward-flowing stream whenever they wanted to go in that direction. As the research vessel continued into the Black Sea, additional new discoveries were made. At a depth of about 300 feet, shells from both saltwater and freshwater shellfish were found in the same locations. Later measurements dated both to the same period of time, about 7,000 years ago. William Ryan and Walter Pitman from Columbia University began to piece the story together.

As the difference in elevation between the Mediterranean and the sunken Black Sea reached its highest point about 7,000 years ago, leaks began to appear in the land bridge. It was the beginning of the end. When the Bosporus land bridge finally gave away soon afterward, the flow of water was huge. One scholar estimated it as 10 cubic miles in the course of a day, 200 times the amount of water that goes through the Niagara gorge daily. The Black Sea is more than 6,000 feet deep so the flow of seawater needed to fill it would be enormous. As it was inundated the water began to spill beyond the level of the surface into the neighboring Mesopotamian region. It was estimated that anyone trying to get away from the rising waters of the Black Sea would probably have to travel half a mile a day in order to keep ahead of the steadily rising flood. Ryan and Pitman subsequently published their conclusions in *Noah's Flood: The New Scientific Discoveries About the Event That Changed History.* Their conclusions caught the attention of Robert Ballard of Titanic fame, long involved in oceanic research. He decided to follow up on the work of Ryan and Pitman with extensive studies inside the Black Sea.

In 1999 and 2000, Ballard discovered an ancient coastline more than 10 miles away from the present Black Sea coast and 300 feet below the surface. On this subterranean shore he found evidence of a former settlement. With the aid of remote-controlled underwater vessels, Ballard's team located a collapsed structure on this ancient coast. Remains of wooden beams that had been worked by human hands were there, along with various stone instruments. The site as a whole was typical of some stone-age settlements that had been unearthed in Turkey. Covering an area today of approximately 600 by 300 miles and reaching depths of more than 6,000 feet, the volume of water that burst through the Bosporus and swept over Mesopotamia must have been immense. Only 300 feet of the Black Sea's present volume of water, the surface part, is fresh. All the rest came from the Mediterranean Sea. Old shipwrecks may yet be found at the bottom of the Black sea, still in pristine condition because they are preserved in the oxygen-free salt water.

Many lives were lost in the devastating flood that overran the area now known as Iraq. Some would have escaped and moved elsewhere. The scattering of people may account for the worldwide records of flood stories. Estimates show that the first rush of water was maintained for about a year, after which lesser flows continued for a further year. In the first year the lake rose about six inches every day and neighboring river valleys were flooded upstream at a rate of a mile a day. Undoubtedly this was the event that gave rise to the story known as Noah's Flood. The fact that it occurred almost 5,000 years before Genesis was written need not surprise anyone. In societies whose records are all oral, events of the magnitude of the Bosporus land bridge destruction stay alive for a long time. There is plenty of evidence of that kind of memory in North American Indian folklore. In the course of time, the memory may well change or be embellished. Given the high quality of the sustained research that Ryan and Pitman obtained, there is every reason to be assured that the events of 7,000 years ago around the Black Sea gave rise, in time, to a more poetic description of it, the one now appearing in Genesis.

SIX

Science Standards
State by State

On August 11, 1999, the Kansas State Board of Education voted 6–4 in favor of removing any mention of biological macroevolution, the age of the Earth, and the origin and early development of the universe in state science standards. It was a bombshell that echoed all across the country. The Associated Press identified it as the top story for the year. Earlier, perhaps due to the influence of the Creation Science Association which influenced the August 11 decision, the Board rejected the views of a 27 member panel of science teachers who wanted to retain the standards that were about to be removed. As a result of the board's vote, evolutionary theory would not appear in state-wide standardized tests and it was left to the 305 local school districts in Kansas whether or not to teach it. It was not long before a nation-wide debate was launched, one that was reminiscent for many of the excesses of the 1920s which culminated in the Scopes Trial. Despite the subsequent decision by Kansas on February 14, 2000, to reinstate normal standards in the science curriculum, a fiery debate had been successfully launched by creationists and their followers. It continues today.

The American Association for the Advancement of Science (AAAS) was the first scientific organization to pass a resolution condemning the Kansas Board's ruling. It added that the decision prevents students from gaining the knowledge and skills they need to succeed in a world that relies increasingly on science and technology. The AAAS also pointed out that the ruling makes it more difficult for Kansas to attract quality science teachers. The Kansas decision of February 2000 was supported by a vote of 7–3. It reinstated the teaching of biological evolution and the origin of the earth into the state's science education standards. Eighth and twelfth grades standards were changed to include reference to the big-bang theory, the understanding of biological evolution, the significance of fossils, and the geologic time scale. Creationists were quick to criticize the revised curriculum and they have continued to do so whenever a state decides either to include the basic Darwinian theory of biological evolution or to make it the only explanation for the development of life forms through the ages. The Kansas Board's favorable action was applauded by many other scientific organizations.

Measuring State Standards

In the year 2000, as a result of the widespread interest generated by the Kansas anachronism, several organizations launched surveys across the country to examine achievements in both the teaching of evolution and in science as a whole. One of the most comprehensive of these was Laurence S. Lerner's. A summary of it is included in Figure 6.1. Lerner examined various aspects of instruction to help him arrive at an overall rating. Under evolution, top marks were given to states that treated evolution in a thorough and detailed manner, and also taught the history of the earth in the light of plate tectonics. Under science standards as a whole, coverage and content as well as the quality of content dominated. By these were meant that coverage and content included the consistent use of experimental and observational methods of study, and for quality the maintenance of unambiguous and appropriate standards. On the negative side, the weakest aspect in the teaching of biological evolution lay in human evolution. Of all the 50 states, only seven make an attempt to include it in measurable detail.

Overall, Lerner found that 31 states did an adequate to excellent job of teaching biological evolution while 19 did a weak to unacceptable performance. Such a poor result is understandable, given that most Americans favor the teaching of both evolution and creationism in science classrooms. Gallup's 1999 poll put the popular

Figure 6.1.
Grades for Treatment of Evolution in Science and for Science Standards as a Whole (Year 2000)

State	Evolution in Science	Science Standards as a Whole
Alabama	F	D
Alaska	D	N/A
Arizona	B	A
Arkansas	D	F
California	A	A
Colorado	B	D
Connecticut	A	B
Delaware	A	A
District of Columbia	B	N/A
Florida	F	F
Georgia	F	F
Hawaii	A	D
Idaho	B	N/A
Illinois	D	B
Indiana	A	A
Iowa	N/A	N/A
Kansas	F	F
Kentucky	D	D
Louisiana	C	C
Maine	F	D
Maryland	C	D
Massachusetts	B	A
Michigan	B	D
Minnesota	B	A
Mississippi	F	
Missouri	B	C
Montana	B	D
Nebraska	C	B
Nevada	C	C
New Hampshire	F	F
New Jersey	A	A
New Mexico	C	F
New York	C	C
North Carolina	A	A

(Grades for Treatment of Evolution in Science, continued)

North Dakota	F	F
Ohio	F	B
Oklahoma	F	F
Oregon	B	B
Pennsylvania	A	N/A
Rhode Island	A	A
South Carolina	A	B
South Dakota	B	B
Tennessee	F	F
Texas	C	C
Utah	B	B
Vermont	B	B
Virginia	D	D
Washington	B	B
West Virginia	F	F
Wisconsin	D	C
Wyoming	F	F

NOTES

N/A = Not available at time of Survey

Evolution in Science		*Science Standards as a Whole*	
A Over 90%	D Over 40%	A Over 95%	D Over 65%
B Over 80%	F Below 40%	B Over 90%	F Below 65%
C Over 60%		C Over 80%	

support at 68 percent. Nevertheless, it is totally wrong to apply democratic principles to matters of scientific fact. The rights of parents do not extend to their acting as experts on either science or the teaching of science. In examining the two sets of grades above, it appears that of the 10 states that received an A for evolution, most of them also received an A for overall science performance and only one received anything below a B. Continuing on to examine developments in the teaching of science over recent years, evidence accumulates that poor performance in science as a whole is usually due to adding the irrelevant question of the origin of life to science classrooms. Chapter One mentions this possibility in the description of Japan's success in the teaching of science.

Whether or not as a result of Lerner's report, some states have been revising upward their standards in science. New Mexico, for example, which for the school year 1997 to 1998 downplayed biological evolution and the age of the earth, has been examining its science curriculum again. On August 28, 2003, by a vote of 13–0, and in the face of intensive efforts by creationists to have their views adopted, the state board of education adopted standards that were wholeheartedly approved by scientific and educational organizations. West Virginia, which received a low grade in the Lerner report, also revised its science curriculum early in 2003. Lerner was asked to comment on the new standards. His evaluation, based on the same criteria he employed in the 2000 report, raised West Virginia's grade to a C. Full marks were awarded for using the word evolution wherever it was warranted. Full marks were also awarded for accurate treatment of geological evolution. There are expectations that other states will raise their standards to bring them into line with established scientific norms.

In 2004, the American Geological Institute (AGI) launched an awareness campaign to alert people across the nation to the widespread attempts by creationists to distort good science education. The institute pointed out that the 1999 Board of Education decision in Kansas brought the evolution debate back into the national spotlight, stimulating a growing number of challenges to the teaching of evolution in state legislatures and school boards around the country. Despite being rebuffed in the courts, creationists still seek to give equal time in classrooms to alternative theories of earth and life history, even including the Biblical account of creation as an historical record. AGI noted that they employ an increasingly popular approach known as **intelligent design** (ID). These efforts fly in the face of science, and it is therefore essential for scientists to inform the public of the scientific method and the importance of the theory of biological evolution. After all, Kansas may have done something good by forcing scientists to improve their communications with the public.

Creationist Interventions in States

Events in different states challenge the public to recognize that the problem of creationists interfering with the teaching of science is not limited to states or school districts. It has reached into the deliberations of Congress, and because of the prestige associated with that body, creationists are making use of senatorial decisions to advance their cause. In the year 2002, as the president's bill No Child Left Behind was moving through Congress, a senator from Pennsylvania introduced an amendment. He proposed adding to the bill the statement, "Biological evolution is a controversial theory." That senator, Rick Santorum, was also supported by Senator Ted Kennedy of Massachusetts. Phillip Johnson, a leader in the creationist movement, had given advice to the Pennsylvanian senator on how his amendment might usefully be worded. Fortunately, there were sufficient senators with scientific backgrounds involved in the bill to prevent the passing of Sanatorum's amendment as an integral part of the bill. It was relegated to a footnote but the fact that it now exists in the final wording of the bill has been exploited by creationists.

Georgia's Department of Education released a new curriculum on January 12, 2004, amid lots of controversy. Middle and high school science standards were proposed by Kathy Cox, the superintendent of schools, in which references to the word evolution would be replaced by the term "biological changes over time." These curriculum changes were developed over 2003 and 2004. While it is not mentioned in the curriculum, Cox said that the new standards could include the teaching of "intelligent design" as another legitimate theory. Scientists and educators are outraged by this plan. Former President Jimmy Carter added that he, as a Christian, a trained engineer, a scientist, and a professor at Emory University, was embarrassed by Superintendent Kathy Cox's attempt to censor and distort the education of Georgia's students.

On April 1, 2003, the Louisiana House of Representatives was presented with a bill, Resolution 50, which was designed to encourage students' thinking skills by refraining from purchasing textbooks that only provide one view of the origin of life. It did not seem to matter that the theory of biological evolution has nothing to do with the origin of life. Here, as in so many other places, the creationists behind the bill insisted that this is what the theory states. The representative who introduced the bill quoted verbatim from the failed amendment to No Child Left Behind as support for his proposal. It is a small step from a bill of this kind, one that will certainly be exploited, to propose that different theories about the origin of life should be included in all science classrooms.

Perhaps the most intriguing as well as extraordinary performances by creationists was the Grand Canyon publication. Every scientist knows well the value of this place when tracing the earth's evolution. The rock-based record exposed in the walls of the canyon spans almost two billion years of earth's history. A visitor to the Grand Canyon on January 8, 2004, was surprised to find a new book in the National Park's bookstores. It asserted that the rocks of the Grand Canyon covered only 6,000 years of earth's history, a record of the only two significant geological events in the history of the earth, Noah's Flood and the six days of creation. The book was titled *Grand Canyon: A Different View*. The compiler of the volume, Thomas Vail, was a river guide for many years and knew every part of the canyon well. The book had 23 co-authors, all male, all a veritable list of who's who in creationism. The format had each chapter beginning with an overview by Vail, followed by brief comments from the other contributors. On the contents pages was a statement as follows, "all contributions have been peer reviewed to ensure a consistent and Biblical perspective."

On July 17, 2003, Michigan's education commissioner, Cheri Pierson Yecke, announced that 41 people had been selected to draft the state's new science standards. This committee of 41 was asked to list specific facts and concepts to cover all the grades from kindergarten to grade 12, and to present their final report to the state legislature at the end of 2004. As has already been seen in relation to Louisiana, Yecke expected to use Santorum's failed amendment to support her personal preference for school districts being free to include creationism. Yecke's personal Biblical convictions are well known. In the same month as Yecke was launching a review of standards in science, Michigan's state legislature was being challenged by two new bills in support of creationism. A large number of legislators supported these bills. Because of this multiple involvement of creationist ideas in a single state, Michigan serves as a good example of how the biological evolution versus creationism conflict

is played out in practice. While considering this attempt by creationists to interfere with good science teaching, note that both the
State Board of Education and the Michigan Science Teachers Association rejected both bills.

One of the July 2003 bills was supported by 26 members of
the legislator and the second one by eight members, altogether quite
a strong lobby for creationists. Contradictions and errors of fact
abound in both bills. In the first bill, for instance, there is an intro-
ductory statement that applies to all of the core curriculum: "The
content standards shall not include attitudes, beliefs, or value systems." Then later, in relation to middle and high school science,
comes the statement, "Indicate that evolution and natural selection
are unproven theories and include that life may be the result of the
purposeful, intelligent design of a Creator." Is it possible for a
teacher to explain this to a group of teenagers who do not believe
anything in the Bible and assure them that the truth of it has nothing to do with belief? In the second bill, the authors recommend
that the popular phrase "design hypothesis" be taught as an explanation for the origin and diversity of life. **Design hypothesis** is
defined as "the theory that life and its diversity result from a com-
bination of chance, necessity, and design." Again, is it possible for
a teacher to teach this with no reference to belief?

In Missouri on December 19, 2003, a bill concerning science
standards in public schools was submitted to the House of Representatives, supported by seven representatives. The bill, which was
passed to the Education Committee for evaluation, proposed that
both biological evolution and **biological intelligent design**—a new
term in the creationist dictionary—be given equal consideration in
the public elementary and secondary schools. The language
employed is interesting, quite in keeping with the ignorance about
science that prevails among creationists. In spite of the almost universal understanding that biological evolution deals only with
changes in life forms over time, coupled with considerable uncertainty as to the mechanisms by which the changes occur, the advocates of this bill assert that it means a theory of the origin of life
and its ascent by naturalistic means. Biological intelligent design,
say the promoters of the bill, is a hypothesis that all species of life

are the result of intelligence. The bill recommends that evolution and design be given equal time in the classroom and that new textbooks must be implemented between 2006 and 2016. They would contain approximately the same number of pages on each of the two views of evolution.

South Carolina's senate passed an education bill on April 29, 2003, that would amend the state's policy regarding the teaching of science. An education committee consisting of two scientists and two physicians was formed to work out the details of the new policy. It was required to take account of three aspects of the teaching of science in schools: (1) To study present standards in science regarding the teaching of the origin of species; (2) To determine whether there is a consensus on the definition of science; (3) To decide whether alternatives to evolution as the origin of species should be offered in schools." The purpose of the new legislation was evident and the American Institute of Biological Sciences was quick to respond. It stated clearly that the bill would undermine South Carolina's strong science tradition and offend science educators and administrators across the state.

After the debacle of the Scopes Trial of 1925 one would expect Tennessee to be the last place enacting new legislation to forbid the teaching of evolution. In fact the state is crystal clear on proper standards for the teaching of biological evolution. Furthermore, according to the state's Commissioner of Education, these high standards are consistently being urged on all school districts. The problem relates to the extensive curricular freedom given to these school districts. On April 15, 2003, Blount County, Tennessee, used its freedom to ban three biology textbooks because they included content about evolution but nothing on creationism. Feelings must have run high because the vote was six to one in favor of the ban. The rejected textbooks had previously been approved at the state level and chosen by most of the state's biology teachers. The science teachers of Blount County will now have to develop a new curriculum, combining evolution and creationism in the biology courses.

Ohio took unusual care in examining public opinion on biological evolution before deciding, at the end of 2002, to recommend new rigorous standards in content that gave no place to creationist thinking. A glance at Lerner's 2000 assessment makes it clear that reform was needed in Ohio. Throughout the year 2002, the state solicited views about the teaching of biological evolution from all across the state. Responses were grouped in four categories as follows:

1. ID. All responses that were against evolution and wanted creationism taught instead. The most common terms employed under this category were intelligent design, intelligent creationism, or creationism.

2. B. These represented the people who wanted to have both evolution and creationism included in the schools' curricula. Similar terms to ID were employed to define creationism.

3. E. The responses that wanted only evolution taught.

4. O. Responses that were happy with existing conditions or just wanted additional information.

Interest must have been high because more than 18,500 responses were received in the course of the year 2002. Strongest support came in category B where close to 13,000 supported that approach. Close to 400 supported ID and 5,000 wanted E. It is to the credit of the state's educational authorities that final curricular decisions rejected the majority view and stayed with the best judgment of scientific experts. This will be discussed in more detail later in this chapter because it is an excellent illustration of the difference between parental democratic rights in education and parental inability to decide appropriate content in specialized areas. Two statements from Ohio's 2002 revised science academic content standards at the grades 9 and 10 level demonstrate the thoroughness with which educational authorities showed their loyalty to scientific expertise: "Explain the 4.5 billion-year-history of earth and the 4 billion-year-history of life on earth based on observable scientific evidence in the geologic record.... Explain the historical and current scientific developments, mechanisms and processes of biological evolution. Describe how scientists continue to investigate and critically analyze these mechanisms and processes."

In sharp contrast to Ohio's scholarly approach, a center in Wyoming made a number of very different decisions. Late in September 2003, the Park County School District in Wyoming decided to permit prayer in school as long as it was not required by a school employee. This decision was part of a range of religious concessions, including freedom to wear religious clothing, display religious symbols, conduct classes in religions as long as no one religion was singled out for endorsement, and permit the teaching of creationism in science classes as one of a number of theories. In another Wyoming center, Washakie County School District, again in 2003, science teachers were permitted to teach alternatives to the theory of evolution. Here, as in so many other places, school board members asserted that evolution was a theory, not a fact, and therefore teachers must be allowed to discuss all scientific theories about the origin of life. The inanity of imposing this kind of academic rigor on grade 9 students, something that would be beyond the capacity of most professional biologists, never seemed to occur to the Washakie board members. Members of the public who attended the board meeting that led to the above decisions were equally blunt in their condemnation of evolution. One person said that it was a product of Hollywood movies and had nothing to do with real science.

Local School Board Autonomy

Wyoming is a good illustration of the problem of raising science standards in schools. Parental groups can pressure local districts when they cannot influence the state. There are quite a few states that give freedom to districts to modify the curriculum as long as they cover the main core content requirements set by the state. Again and again educational authorities report that the problem of school district freedom is a major irritant in attempts to raise standards in science. Typical of the situations are comments like this from one supervisor who traveled the state to help raise standards in the teaching of science: "I find that teachers are not interested in what I have to say. They are determined to make peace with local parental groups when these people insist on including creationism.

It makes life much easier for them." The inability to exercise control over standards at the school district level stems from long-standing custom and is standard practice in Indiana, Kentucky, Louisiana, and Virginia, among others. In South Dakota, the words biological evolution are rarely used and never defined. Arizona has no position paper or other document regarding the teaching of evolution. Given the sensitivity of politicians to public opinion, citizens are not likely to see in the foreseeable future, at the state level, new laws requiring good science in every classroom.

The U.S. constitution makes no provision for the control of education. Hence, by custom, all such control lies within the states. No single tradition in public education is more deeply rooted than local control over the operation of schools. Local autonomy has long been thought essential both to the maintenance of community concerns and the maintenance of the quality of education. Some argue that it is the bedrock of the country's greatness just as the free market and capitalism are the foundations of economic strength. It is argued that people are more productive when they have a vested interest. Circumstantially, there are historical reasons for this devotion to local autonomy and, once entrenched, schools and school districts are reluctant to lose that autonomy. U.S. high school total enrolment in 1890 was less than 400,000. By 1910 it was over a million and, in 1930, it had reached five million. The early years of the twentieth century were marked by huge increases in the numbers of immigrants. To meet their educational needs schools sprang up all over the country, large numbers of them so remote from state capitals that they had to cope locally for all their needs.

New initiatives appear and reappear in modern times from state and federal agencies, reducing the powers of school districts. Sometimes they are due to the distribution of new federal or state grants of money, all of which normally carry performance standards as conditions for receiving the grants. Statewide exams and teacher certification requirements are other examples. On occasion, as in 2004, the state governor of Illinois proposed that he have direct oversight of the state's schools. The problem of maintaining high standards of achievement in science is likely to be one more reason for external interference with the traditional rights of school boards. As indicated previously, in light of parental pressures, it seems almost certain that a high quality of achievement in science education will only occur if state authorities exercise much greater control over the day to day activities in all science classrooms. Democratic decisions are made by citizens about who will represent them in deciding educational policy and expenditures. This is exactly as it should be. It applies at the school board level and at state level. It does not apply to determining the work of individual teachers or defining the specialized content they teach. For example, the date of the Pearl Harbor attack of December 7, 1941, is not determined by parental vote. It is a fact of history. School districts across the U.S. vary greatly in the numbers of students for which they are responsible. The average is a little over 700 per district but the range is from more than a million (New York City Public Schools) to just a few students. Outside help has become essential for the bigger ones.

One revolutionary loss of power was experienced by all school districts at the height of political action for civil rights in the 1950s and 1960s. Desegregation became the order of the day and schools were compelled to adjust whether they wanted to or not. This was how Chief Justice Earl Warren of the U.S. Supreme Court put it on 17 May 1954: "We come then to the question presented: Does segregation of children in public schools solely on the basis of race, even though the physical facilities and other 'tangible' factors may be equal, deprive the children of the minority group of equal educational opportunities? We believe that it does. We conclude that in the field of public education the doctrine of 'separate but equal' has no place. Separate educational facilities are inherently unequal. Therefore, we hold that the plaintiffs and others similarly situated for whom the actions have been brought are, by reason of the segregation complained of, deprived of the equal protection of the laws guaranteed by the Fourteenth Amendment." The Court's decision was known as *Brown v. Board of Education* and it cast an iron grip on all matters of segregation for more than 30 years.

Then, 38 years after *Brown v. the Board of Education,* the DeKalb County School Board (based on San Diego) had an interesting outcome when it opposed racial integration and launched an appeal. In 1992 Justice Scalia of the U.S. Supreme Court, supported by a majority, said the following: "Our decision will be of great assistance to the citizens of DeKalb County who for the first time since 1969 will be able to run their own public schools, at least so far as student assignments are concerned. It will have little effect, however, upon the many other school districts throughout the country that are still being supervised by federal judges, since it turns upon the extraordinarily rare circumstance of a finding that no portion of the current racial imbalance is a remnant of prior de jure discrimination. While it is perfectly appropriate for the Court to decide this case on that narrow basis, we must resolve—if not today, then soon—what is to be done in the vast majority of other districts, where, though our cases continue to profess that judicial oversight of school operations is a temporary expedient, democratic processes remain suspended, with no prospect of restoration."

Almost a quarter century ago this Court held that school systems which had been enforcing de jure segregation at the time of Brown had not merely an obligation to assign students and resources on a race neutral basis but also an "affirmative duty" to "desegregate," that is, to achieve insofar as practicable racial balance in their schools. This holding has become such a part of the country's legal fabric that there is a tendency, reflected in the Court of Appeals opinion in this case, to speak as though the Constitution requires such racial balancing. Of course it does not: The Equal Protection Clause reaches only those racial imbalances shown to be intentionally caused by the State. The sole question in school desegregation cases is one of remedies for past violations. Returning schools to the control of local authorities at the earliest practicable date is essential to restore their true accountability in our governmental system. So the to and fro of tension over control of local school boards continues. In spite of the reassuring judgment rendered by Justice Scalia, school boards know that new intrusions from state and federal authorities will continue to appear.

Creationists' Belief Systems

Chapter One described creationists in terms of their various viewpoints on creationism. These different positions continue to reappear in the various events listed previously. But who are the people who hold these convictions? Are they an identifiable group within America and what would they say if they were asked about their beliefs? Do they represent particular churches or societies or are they an amorphous group of people who might be found in churches and other meeting places anywhere and everywhere? Fortunately it is now possible to identify the vast majority of them through their loyalty to a widely used statement of faith. They are evangelicals, people who identify with a movement that came to strength in the Western world over the past 200 years. In the United States, over the course of the twentieth century, they rose to a more dominant position in the Christian community. In the 1970s and 1980s Gallup polls identified them as 34 percent of the American population and 47 percent in the 1990s. Gallup's method was to ask sample populations, "Would you describe yourself as a born again or evangelical Christian?" Their statistics emerge from that question.

In Britain, over the second half of the twentieth century, the common bonds among evangelicals were encouraged by Christian leaders and led to the emergence of several organizations, each dedicated to unity of purpose and action. Christian college unions, Christian high school organizations, and the Evangelical Alliance were visible evidences of the new emphasis. Loyalty to the gospel as defined by foundational statements of faith became the watchword of the day. A higher loyalty was demanded than that due to particular churches or denominations. Interdenominationalism and par-church organizations were phrases and names in common use. Unity became more important than doctrine. Keswick Convention, a long-standing annual interdenominational meeting, was specially suited to this new unity drive. It's motto had always been "All One in Christ Jesus."

A large number of American evangelicals are known as the Religious Right because of their increasingly active involvement in state and federal politics. They constitute a powerful force in the political life of the country. They are the evangelicals who would not be sympathetic to the words of Professor Johan Heyns, moderator of South Africa's Dutch Reformed Church, who pointed out after apartheid had finally been abandoned, "We never again want temporal power. We made such a mess of it when we had it." Alongside these more militant evangelicals is a range of others who share the same belief system as the Religious Right but who see the practical outworking of their faith in a variety of different kinds of activities. Furthermore their lives cut across all the traditional academic, social, and religious divisions. David Bebbington, in *Evangelicalism in Modern Britain: A History from the 1730s to the 1980s*, summarizes their essential beliefs as he found them expressed throughout these two centuries. Readers can look at his statements briefly and then compare them with a present day statement of faith, one that is supported by the vast majority of evangelicals.

Bebbington traces the origin of evangelicals to the churches arising from the Reformation in the sixteenth and seventeenth centuries. Yet the usage of the word from the eighteenth century onward was quite non-partisan. People were reluctant to apply it to any one group. Four ISMS, in Bebbington's mind, flowed consistently through the times he documents and these were the qualities that defined evangelicalism. They were conversionism, activism, biblicism, and crucicentrism. By conversionism he meant turning away from one way of living, the selfcentered way, to a surrender to Jesus Christ and a receiving of his forgiveness. There was a parting of the ways at this stage with the old Roman Catholic Church and those that retained its traditions, particularly the one that required church baptism as essential to true conversion. Evangelicals completely rejected that requirement. Activism implied prayer and selfless service to one's neighbor. Biblicism meant the supreme authority of the Bible, under God, for the Christian's guidance. All evangelicals agreed that it was inspired by God. All the arguments began at that point, dividing evangelicals into a plethora of camps based on different interpretations. Crucicentrism, unlike the other four, had an ineradicable visual double symbol, a man on a Roman cross and, then, an empty tomb. The cross thereby became the enduring symbol of evangelical faith and life and the heart of the gospel.

In modern America, the evangelical movement is represented by the twice-monthly journal, *Christianity Today*. It is the expression of the evangelical community. It's more than 200 staff, editors, and advisors are very representative of the whole movement. In 2004 it celebrated its fiftieth anniversary with observations like the following: evangelicals have become dominant because they contribute to a new style of ecumenism, even though minorities still remain separatist-minded. They have also moved from what was a kind of private Protestantism to easy identification with the prevailing culture. They have adapted more readily than others to the main lines of American life. They sing the battle hymns of the republic and even endorse warfare. Once upon a time they were known as the godliness-with-contentment people. Today they are completely at home with theological justifications for the stock market and globalism. Amid all of this present day reality, one might be surprised by the conservative nature of its 50-year-old and still strong statement of faith. Here are the seven parts of the evangelical statement of faith:

A. The 66 canonical books of the Bible as originally written were inspired of God, hence free from error. They constitute the only infallible guide in faith and practice.

B. There is one God, the Creator and Preserver of all things, infinite in being and perfection. He exists eternally in three Persons: the Father, the Son, and the Holy Spirit, who are of one substance and equal in power and glory.

C. God created Adam and Eve in his own image. By disobedience, they fell from their sinless state through the temptation by Satan. This fall plunged humanity into a state of sin and spiritual death, and brought upon the entire race the sentence of eternal death. From this condition we can be saved only by the grace of God, through faith, on the basis of the work of Christ, and by the agency of the Holy Spirit.

D. The eternally pre-existent Son became incarnate without human father, by being born of the Virgin Mary. Thus, in the Lord Jesus Christ, divine and human natures were united in one Person, both natures being whole, perfect, and distinct. To effect salvation, he lived a sinless life and died on the cross as the sinner's substitute, shedding his blood for the remission of sins. On the third day he rose from the dead in the body which had been laid in the tomb. He ascended to the right hand of the Father, where he performs the ministry of intercession. He shall come again, personally and visibly, to complete his saving work and to consummate the eternal plan of God.

E. The Holy Spirit is the third Person of the Triune God. He applies to man the work of Christ. By justification and adoption we are given a right standing before God; by regeneration, sanctification, and glorification our nature is renewed.

F. When we have turned to God in penitent faith in the Lord Jesus Christ, we are accountable to God for living a life separated from sin and characterized by the fruit of the Spirit. It is our responsibility to contribute by word and deed to the universal spread of the Gospel.

G. At the end of the age, the bodies of the dead shall be raised. The righteous shall enter into full possession of eternal bliss in the presence of God, and the wicked shall be condemned to eternal death.

Statements of faith like this one, coupled with the variety of interpretations of the Bible already referred to give rise to a pluralism in the evangelical community that is unmatched in any other faith or religious organization. Over and over again writers seem to subscribe to these seven statements yet continue to write at polar distances from any middle ground as to their meanings. Some statements by theologians discuss the six days of the cosmos' creation in Genesis in which each day lasts for 24 hours as known today. Others seem to be on the side of Galileo, defending science against the church by affirming the unity of the two books of God, Bible and Nature, but then asserting that Adam and Eve were the first living humans. At the more enlightened end of the spectrum there are writers who love both Bible and science and welcome every contribution from the latter. The American Scientific Affiliation, a Christian organization dedicated to a better understanding of the relevance of scientific discoveries, has gone a step further than the Roman Catholic Church. In contrast to the latter which declares that only some aspects of humans came from the earliest forms of life, it states clearly that biological evolution, the common descent of all living things, is well-supported by diverse lines of experimental evidence.

It is rare to find scholars who are as familiar with theology as they are with science. There are a few and they are the ones who are the best exponents of a healthy evangelical perspective on the facts of science as well as the meaning of the Bible. Here are some of the kinds of statements that come from them: "There certainly is a problem with human nature. Hopes get crushed and human desires are frequently misdirected into destructive activities. While this is true, no responsible scientist can believe that these conditions are due to a single disastrous act on the part of one person among our ancestors. In all probability, struggles developed in hominid lines as they evolved into *Homo sapiens.* As they discovered their dependence on their creator, coupled with a spiritual awareness of his presence, a challenge came with that discovery. It said, in effect, shall we recognize our dependency or shall we turn away from the creator to find self sufficiency in ourselves? Thus was human autonomy asserted over creaturely dependence and succeeding generations followed suit."

SEVEN

The Evolution of Intelligent Design

Chapter Six described the leaders in the U.S. evangelical community. Most of them are opposed to the theory of evolution. This chapter will add some information on the people involved directly or via various organizations in the creationist movement and whose work has led to the recent emphasis on intelligent design. Some are from the U.S., some from other countries. Many of them will share the same views as those described in the evangelical movement.

The starting point is 1957. In September of that year the old Soviet Union launched Sputnik around the world and woke up America to the threat that its achievements in science were inferior. The U.S. National Science Foundation funded science projects for schools almost at once in order to raise standards. One of the first to reach widespread acceptance was the Biological Sciences Curriculum Study (BSCS). Early in the 1960s it was in use across the country and its acceptance of the theory of evolution as fact triggered numerous new reactions from creationists. Little interest had been expressed about evolution since the days of the Scopes trial, mainly because of the confusion arising from the outcome of that event. Celebrations over the hundredth anniversary of Darwin's work in 1959 strengthened further the latent opposition to all that was represented by evolution.

The names here represent the dominant views of creationists in three time periods, before and after 1957, and in the 1990s and early 2000s.

The name of George McCready Price (1870–1963) should first

145

be mentioned, even though he represents opposition to evolution at a much earlier date. The reason for this is because his views, old though they were, persisted well beyond his death through others who picked up where he left off. This was a rare achievement for a creationist. For the most part, as already noted in Chapter One, there are many viewpoints within the creationist camp and few last more than a decade or two. Changing social, scientific, legal and political developments compel them to change the terms and the tactics they use. Some of the more recent writers refuse to identify with the word creationist because of its changing meanings over the years. However, for most of the twentieth century, creationism, or creation science, defined the activities of the vast majority who opposed evolution in schools. Most of the space in this chapter will be given to people from the last of the three time periods identified, the contemporary phase known as intelligent design.

George McCready Price

George Price was brought up in a Seventh Day Adventist church in Canada, and from these Adventist beginnings he had a particular devotion to the keeping of the Sabbath, the seventh day of the week. In Adventist theology, Christian values are celebrated on Saturday because that was the law in Old Testament times. Thus Price was particularly devoted to the idea that the early part of Genesis, the record of six days as we understand them today, must be defended in order to be faithful to scripture. He was a prolific writer and his first major book, *Outlines of Modern Christianity and Modern Science*, appeared in 1902. He called it the first attempt to take the Biblical side of the science versus religion controversy. This book focused on geology, a subject which he proposed to reconstruct on the basis of events described in the Bible. The central focus in his view of things was a recent creation and one catastrophic event, Noah's flood.

Based on the flood, he concluded that just about everything imaginable in geology had been a consequence of that one event which he saw as affecting the entire globe. He explained the presence of many fossils as having been deposited in various places when the flood reshaped the surface of the earth, and he attributed a great deal of the present day surface to a huge wind that followed the flood. He saw in this one event the destruction of large forests as they were swept away with the wind and the accompanying flood and deeply buried so that, in time, they would be turned into the coal and oil that we discover today. Mountains, such as the Alps and Himalayas, which are known to have sedimentary rocks at their summits, he saw as deposits laid down by the worldwide flood and later uplifted. He regarded the Earth as completely without life before the narrative found in the first few chapters of the book of Genesis. When he encountered overlapping strata in rocks, he insisted that they had to be laid down at the same time. So in general he was devoted to the literal interpretation of the early part of Genesis and therefore to a very young earth.

Price had little to say about fossils and the history of life. He felt that the study of geology in light of the Bible would explain everything. He explained that the Niagara River gorge and the Grand Canyon were carved out by the flood before the sedimentary elements had completely hardened and he dismissed any idea of an ice age as the wildest dream ever imported into science. Volcanic action and earthquakes he interpreted as due to the ignition of coal deposits underground. Perhaps the most imaginative part of Price's geology was his suggestion that a shift in the earth's axis released massive volumes of water from subterranean reservoirs. He may have borrowed that idea from Thomas Burnet's writings in an earlier century. His one detailed reference to fossils described them as the buried remains of animals killed in the flood. All forms of life would be distributed according to their specific gravities with humans nearest the surface since they would have reached higher ground before being engulfed.

He became well known because of his many writings, especially following the publication in 1923 of what he called his main work, *The New Geology*. He was generally regarded as the main scientific authority amongst the various fundamentalist Christians. When the Scopes trial took place in Tennessee, the person who was defending Creationism, William Jennings Bryan, was anxious to bring him in as an authority, but he was unfortunately in England at that time.

Price's influence on another person who picked up his concepts about Noah's flood leads into the second period of time. It is dominated by Henry M. Morris, the most influential voice in creationism from 1960 to 1990. Morris and John C. Whitcomb Jr. wrote a book in 1961, *The Genesis Flood: The Biblical Record and its Scientific Implications*, which was published by the Presbyterian and Reformed Publishing Company in Philadelphia. This book made its appearance at the end of what might be called the long silence, the more than 30 years following the Scopes trial when few wanted to do anything about either evolution or creationism. That all changed after Sputnik, and Morris was one of the first to act against the new status given to evolution by the Biological Sciences Curriculum Study.

Henry M. Morris

Morris's book picked up from the work of George Price and made it a little more up to date in some areas, but fundamentally it was the same thesis, that Noah's flood explained a great deal of the events that occurred on the surface of the earth over the entire historical period. Like Price, Morris and Whitcomb Jr. discarded any idea of uniformity in geological history. In six literal days, they asserted, using methods that as yet are not understood, God had created the entire universe and populated the earth with fully-grown plants, animals and humans. Evidence was adduced that humans and dinosaurs had lived together at the same time. Human footprints alongside those of dinosaurs, even a dinosaur track superimposed on a human one had been found, they claimed. The Fall of Adam and Eve, they said, had introduced decay and deterioration to a world that had been perfect. All the rock strata with their fossils had to post date this event. It all happened within the last 6,000 years.

Within its first decade the book sold tens of thousands of copies and over the following 15 years an additional 150,000. Morris and Whitcomb Jr. became famous sought-after speakers and authors. Strict creationists were delighted to have a book that made catastrophism respectable while scientists scorned it. The controversy over its accuracy added more sales. Most of the evangelical journals were interested in it but few gave it their full support. Morris visited and spoke at churches and theological colleges all over America. Many of the more conservative ones invited him to join their faculties. At Bob Jones University, where two of Morris' sons were enrolled, the administration offered to put him in charge of a new department of apologetics. At Dallas Theological Seminary, the largest nondenominational conservative seminary in the world, his lecture on "Biblical Cosmology and Modern Science" was received enthusiastically with students giving him a standing ovation at the end of the lecture.

Two years after the appearance of *The Genesis Flood,* Morris along with several others formed the Creation Research Society. Its statement of belief was a clear recognition of majority creationism at that time, a belief that remained strong for most of them throughout the 1970s and 1980s. It had five components, all of them binding on all members of the society. The first and second say, "(1) The Bible is the written Word of God, and because it is inspired throughout, all its assertions are historically and scientifically true in all the original autographs. To the student of nature this means that the account of origins in Genesis is a factual presentation of simple historical truths; (2) All basic types of living things, including man, were made by direct creative acts of God during the creation week described in Genesis. Whatever biological changes have occurred since creation week have accomplished only changes within the original created kinds."

The statement of belief continues with "(3) The great flood described in Genesis, commonly referred to as the Noachian flood, was an historic event worldwide in its extent and effect; (4) We are an organization of Christian men of science who accept Jesus Christ as our Lord and Savior. The account of the special creation of Adam and Eve as one man and woman and their subsequent fall into sin is the basis for our belief in the necessity of a savior for all mankind. Therefore, salvation can come only through accepting Jesus Christ as our savior." As a postscript to the statement of belief there was a declaration that no publication of the society would ever advocate an old earth or geological-ages position.

In the course of the 1970s and 1980s the term "flood geology" gave way to "creation science" or "scientific creationism" so that schools could teach the basic scientific creation model without reference to the Bible. In reality little had changed for most creationists from the centuries-old flood geology views of Price.

Kenneth A. Ham

As we consider the third period of time, the 1990s and early 2000s, we find the face of creationism going through a fundamental change. No longer was the focus on a young earth and different interpretations of the historical content of Genesis. Disputes with established scientific facts faded and several creationist leaders happily accepted the four plus billion years of the earth's age along with a much greater age for the rest of the universe. The new phrase that came into vogue and very soon emerged as the defining label was **intelligent design**. It was and is a very old idea in its essential meaning and has already been identified it in its older form as natural theology. As will be seen, the majority of the creationist leaders in this third period are advocates of intelligent design. There are one or two leaders who are presently active and subscribe to the older views and Kenneth A. Ham is one of them. He is included here to provide a transition from such earlier creationists as Henry Morris.

Kenneth Ham comes from Australia. He is the Executive Director of an organization called Answers in Genesis. He was educated in Australia and holds Bachelor's and Master's degrees from there, and is a former teacher in that country. He is very much a part of the young earth creationists. Similar to Henry Morris in that regard, he sees the earth as little more than 6,000 years old, and he holds that position with a criticism of radiometric methods of dating rocks, which he says is not reliable. His view of Genesis is interesting because he argues that Christian leaders through the centuries have accepted the notion that secular notions are right and true, even when they are opposed to the biblical account of creation. From that he concludes that many of the social problems we encounter today are due to a neglect of the absolute authority of the Bible. This is a view that is very popular today. It has been covered previously here and noted in much of the opposition to the teaching of biological evolution in the schools. The conclusion of many is that without the absolute authority of the Bible, morality will disappear and there will be no law in communities other than that of the jungle.

For quite a long period of time from the late 1980s to the mid 1990s, Kenneth Ham was associated with the Institute for Creation Research in the United States, which incidentally is said to be the largest creationist organization in the world. During that time he strongly defended his view of the role of the bible. At an earlier point, in 1989, he published a book called *The Lie: Evolution*, which is focused on the argument that evolution cannot be made to fit the biblical account. As recently as early 2004, in a U.S. lecture, he traced the traditional views of creationists, the notion of six days of creation being extended periods of time, and the gap theory relating to the first one or two verses of the first chapter of Genesis. Ham insisted that these were steps by theologians through history in their rejection of biblical authority. He saw the first weakness as attributing the six days of creation to very long periods of time. Then the second weakness was rejecting the authority of scripture in the gap theory. Ham then concluded that nowadays, because of these weaknesses through the years, the Darwinian theory can be taught as part of Bible study.

By the late 1990s Ham was reaching most of the United States from a base in Cincinnati through 500 radio stations. His messages were directed to young people and they were backed up by books and videos. With a multi-million dollar annual budget his work is bigger than most creationist ventures. He points out that, because the earth is only thousands of years old, humans must have lived at the same time as dinosaurs. All of Ham's activities occur outside most churches and religious organizations but it is evident that he has the support of a very large number of people.

Upon leaving the arena of traditional creationists and considering the intelligent design leaders, discussion frequently shifts from facts to philosophy. This is the case with the first person considered, Michael Behe. Ordinarily, philosophical questions are irrelevant to the purpose of this book, which deals with getting better standards of science in the schools, but philosophers of intelligent design are likewise keenly interested in interfering with school science programs.

Michael J. Behe

Michael Behe is professor of biochemistry at Lehigh University and author of *Darwin's Black Box: The Biochemical Challenge to Evolution*. He is a member of the Biophysical Society and also of the American Society for Molecular Biology and Biochemistry. The title of his book is drawn from a statement by Darwin along the following lines: "If it could be demonstrated that any complex organ existed which could not possibly have been formed by numerous, successive, slight modifications, my theory would absolutely break down." Behe picks up on this statement and argues that the most convincing evidence for design is not to be found in the stars or the fossils, but in biochemical systems. He goes on to say that any system that is irreducibly complex is one where the removal of one of its parts causes the whole system to cease functioning. He picks the common mousetrap as an illustration of one such system. Any system of this kind, says Behe, cannot be produced directly by numerous, successive, slight modifications. Natural selection can only choose systems that are already working as complete wholes, so a biological system would have to arise as an integrated unit for natural selection to be able to act on it.

Behe's book was very popular because it seemed to cast serious doubt on the theory of evolution and, at the same time, to demonstrate the necessity of a creator, a designer of life. The evangelical publication *Christianity Today*, honored him with their book of the year award in 1997, the year after it was published. Behe was greatly influenced by the writings of other creationists but he is far removed from the leaders of the 1960s and before. He is not devoted to the idea of a very young Earth, nor is he critical of the basic Darwinian theory of evolution. He is quite happy with the concept of the universe being billions of years old and all life on earth having a common origin. While his book was a bestseller and was widely accepted by the community of people opposed to Darwin's theory, the book, unfortunately, was based on Darwin's notion of natural selection, a view of the mechanisms involved in the evolution of life that of course is no longer universally held. Darwin was by no means competent in regard to understanding the mechanisms that caused evolution. He was quite clear about the fact that all life emerged from a common origin, but the paths by which life changed were not known in his time, as was discussed in Chapter Four. Unfortunately, it is not uncommon to find people like Behe building theories on indefensible premises.

Behe is an advisory board member of the Intelligent Design and Evolution Awareness Centre in San Diego, which was established in the year 2001, and is dedicated to the priority of intelligent design theory. In his book, *Darwinism Comes to America*, Ronald Numbers quotes from Michael Behe's book and also from a subsequent interview regarding that book, indicating that Behe thought of his book as pushing Darwin's theory to the limit by opening the ultimate black box, the cell, thereby making possible the understanding of how life works. Behe goes on to say the astonishing complexity of sub-cellular organic structure led him to conclude, on the basis of scientific data, not from sacred books or sectarian beliefs, that intelligent design had been at work. So Behe is anxious to separate himself from any defense of Genesis. Instead, he is saying that he has established his views on the basis of scientific data. Behe even says that the result is so unambiguous and so significant that it must be ranked as one of the greatest achievements in the history of science. This is an extraordinary statement to make, but according to Numbers, this is exactly what was said, that this discovery rivals those of Newton and Einstein and Pasteur, and even Darwin.

These are levels of arrogance that do not belong to the best traditions of science. Intellectual humility is the cardinal virtue in that domain. Newton and the others worked with real world data as the basis for their discoveries. Behe is working with ideas that cannot be validated by experiments. Furthermore, when a leader in the field of intelligent design makes statements like those above, his ideas get picked up by lesser lights as authoritative information.

That happened with Nancy Pearcey in *Signs of Intelligence* when she wrote that design is poised to revolutionize science as dramatically as Newtonian physics did in its day. It would also be helpful if leaders like Behe could show greater respect for some of the well-established theories of science such as the age of the earth and the basic Darwinian theory as distinct from its mechanisms. Edward Larson points out that Behe saw the disreputable decisions of 1999 in Kansas as heartening. What could he mean by that?

William A. Dembski

William Dembski is a research professor in the Conceptual Foundations of Science at Baylor University. He is also a senior Fellow with the Discovery Institute's Centre for the Renewal of Science and Culture which is located in Seattle. Dembski is a Christian philosopher of science who, along with some others, has contributed to the new publication of the intelligent design people, *Origins and Designs*, which was launched in the 1990s. He is also the Executive Director of the International Society for Complexity Information and Design, a U.S. non-profit organization dedicated to the study of complex systems. One of the interesting aspects of Dembski's work is its separation from Christian views of the universe. He feels that many non–Christians are involved in the study of intelligent design, although his personal position is as a Christian philosopher of science. Amongst Dembski's books are the following: *Designing Science: Eliminating Chance Through Small Probabilities*; *No Free Lunch: Why Specified Complexity Cannot Be Purchased Without Intelligence*; and *Intelligent Design: The Bridge Between Science and Theology*.

Dembski is a strong supporter of Behe's work. As a philosopher-mathematician he suggested that there are certain standards by which one can identify intelligent design. These include the consideration of contingency (which means chance), specification (which means laws), and complexity. It is the evidence of complexity that gives strong support to the notion of intelligent design. Like others in the intelligent design movement, Dembski prefers not to identify with the word creationism because of its many different meanings. He prefers to describe himself as a Christian philosopher of science with a particular interest in intelligent design. He believes that God created the world but he does not regard Genesis as a scientific document. He can readily accept that the Earth is more than four billion years old and that the universe is three times that age. He insists, like the scientists studied in the earlier part of this book, that science and scripture do not contradict each other.

Scholars such as Behe and Dembski are at the core of the intelligent design movement and because of their scholarship credentials they attract people who would never have taken an interest in the older creationist models. Some people use the phrase "the new creationism" for their work, particularly because of Dembski's emphasis that non–Christians can be involved. As already seen, it is the intelligent design argument that appears most frequently among legislators who propose adding creationism to school science. Scientists are not so kind to the work of these two scholars. Richard Dawkins calls it intellectually dishonest. He thinks that a cowardly flabbiness of the intellect afflicts otherwise rational people when they are confronted with long-standing religions. Kenneth Miller, an evolutionary biologist, dismissed intelligent design as an imposter masquerading as a scientific theory.

Michael J. Denton

Michael Denton is a molecular biologist at the University of Otago, New Zealand. He is not a biblical creationist and describes himself as an evolutionist. He is often regarded as the person who laid the intellectual foundations for the intelligence design (ID) movement. That may be due to his book published in 1986 called, *Evolution: Theory in Crisis*. Denton regarded a book by Phillip E. Johnson, a person who will be covered later in this chapter, as the single best critique of Darwinism that he had ever read. He became deeply involved in the intelligent design movement substantially as a result of that influence. Denton has also written another book more recently called, *Nature's Destiny: How the Laws of Biology Reveal Purpose in the Universe*. That book, published in 1998, took a very different view of nature and the cosmos. In Denton's mind, it is entirely what is described as an anthropomorphic story. That's a term that is used when one says that things refer specifically to human life.

Denton argued that the entire cosmos is a specially designed whole thing with life and humanity as its single goal and purpose. In other words, all aspects of reality, from the size of galaxies to the boiling point of water, are designed for this one goal. The interesting thing about this anthropomorphic view of the universe is that scientists will say something similar. In their view, everything forms part of a single unity of purpose of form. They would see this unity of purpose as a natural phenomena because human reason can look at the universe and see its coordinated whole. Thus, rather like Dembski's view of the Bible and intelligent design, so Denton's view could be conceived as two views from different vantage points. Denton is a member of the editorial advisory board of the publication, *Origins and Designs*. Unfortunately, like others in similar enthusiasm for intelligent design, Denton selects a view of Darwinian evolution that has nothing to do with the theory of evolution and is not scientifically defensible in order to make a case for ID. He stated that the essential bedrock of Darwinism is that all the organisms that have ever existed were generated by the accumulation of entirely undirected mutations. Every evolutionist would reject that assertion.

Phillip E. Johnson

Phillip Johnson is a former law professor, a conservative criminal law expert at the University of California at Berkeley. His publication in 1991, *Darwin on Trial*, gave a strong impetus to the ID movement, which was just beginning at that time. Johnson has remained one of its leading exponents ever since. His book in 1991 was triggered by reading Richard Dawkins' book, *The Blind Watchmaker*, in which Dawkins makes the unfortunate comment that modern biology justifies atheism. There is no excuse for that kind of statement. It's totally unjustified, and all responsible scientists would say so. Unfortunately, some scientists do overstep the mark and go beyond their field of expertise. This book of Johnson's was so successful that the governor of Alabama sent copies to every biology teacher across the state. Johnson's second book, *Reason in the Balance: The Case Against Naturalism in Science, Law and Education* was published in 1995 and was equally well received.

The problem with Johnson, as with so many others in ID, is that a phrase or a word is taken out of context, or is not correct in the first place, and a whole argument is built on it. For example, in the case of Johnson, he makes the statement that material entities subject to physical laws account for everything in nature. He says that this is claimed by scientists. He does not indicate which scientists he had in mind, perhaps because it might be very difficult to find one to support his statement. On this totally unsubstantiated statement he then proceeds to build a case against evolution. If only he had read the last words of Darwin in *The Origin of Species*, he would know how false was his basic premise: "This view of life, having been originally breathed by the Creator into a few forms or into one." Thus Johnson builds up his case about naturalistic limits of thought.

The other assumption that Johnson makes in his writings is that the theory of evolution is based on Darwin's suggestion that natural selection was the mechanism that determined changes through the history of life. It is now known, as outlined in Chapter Four, that Darwin was not correct in making that assumption. His expertise lay in the basic theory of evolution about the common origin of all forms of life, but he was not an expert on the mechanisms involved. Subsequently, it has been discovered that there are many mechanisms affecting the transformation of life forms. People like Johnson capitalize on something that is a weakness and has subsequently been corrected but, because Darwin had written it, they feel that they can build a case on it.

Another illustration of the way in which experts tend to go beyond their field of competence is illustrated in the way that Johnson refers to the outlook of biological evolutionists. In universities and in schools of training, he says, the history of life belongs to evolutionary biology. This assignment of authority implies that the question of how living organisms came into existence is a matter of specialized knowledge, knowledge that is not available to persons outside the inner circle of science. This is quite wrong. No evolutionary biologist claims any knowledge whatsoever about the origin of life.

It is this habit amongst the ID people of picking on things that are not an integral part of true science, and building a case on it, that causes the difficulties for mutual understanding. These various claims that are so unwarranted, namely that naturalism is the only legitimate way of doing science, and then going beyond the bounds of science to focus on conditions for which scientists have not expertise, such as the origin of life, is a big part of the difficulty of getting understanding between the two worlds of science and Christian faith.

When the Kansas Board of Education in 1999 abolished the references to evolution and the great age of the earth, Johnson described the Board's decision as courageous. Why? Everyone knows it was a totally unsupportable decision. As a result, Johnson found himself among the political leaders of that time who supported the Kansas decision for crass political gain.

Of even greater significance was Johnson's interference with a bill going through the U.S. Congress, the famous education bill "No Child Left Behind." According to Edward J. Larson, Senator Rick Santorum of Pennsylvania, who wanted to introduce an amendment to that bill, had Phillip Johnson help him draft it. Fortunately, Santorum was unable to have his amendment entered within the bill because there were enough senators who knew a little about the theory of evolution. The amendment was added as a footnote to the bill and ever since, because of the prestige of any senate document, that note has been quoted by ID advocates in their attacks on school science. The actual wording of Santorum's addition was, "Where biological evolution is taught, the curriculum should help students to understand why this subject generates so much continuing controversy." In recent years, several states have been presented with ID bills proposing shared treatment of creationism and evolution, and in each case the Santorum note is adduced for support.

Dean H. Kenyon

Dean Kenyon is a senior biology professor at San Francisco State University and his publications have brought a different aspect

158

of ID to the fore. In fact, his work is not a subject that belongs to the main theme of this book because it focuses on the origin of life, which is not a part of the theory of evolution. However, because he is so much involved with the ID movement it is wise to mention him. He wrote a book called *Pandas and People: The Central Question of Biological Origins.* It was a small book of six case studies in which the evolutionary point of view and the ID one were placed side by side. The intention was that schools could give space to both views of the origins of life and decide, in the process, which was the better. Predictably, the ID seemed to come out ahead every time, and it was not long before the few schools that were using the book lost interest in it.

ID, the new creationism as some call it, is the latest and probably final manifestation of anti-evolutionism. It pretends to be a science but it has no credibility within the scientific community because it lacks the scientific method. For example, leaders such as Michael J. Behe, William A. Dembski, and Phillip E. Johnson formulated their recently published ideas as a criticism of some questionable aspects of Darwin's 1859 proposition. They ignored in the process all the subsequent scientific research that built on the original work. Today, the Darwinian theory of evolution receives universal acclaim and enjoys the support of an impressive array of other scientific disciplines such as geology, molecular biology, physical anthropology, and biochemistry.

EIGHT

Models of Biological Science Curricula

In concluding this study of the conflicts over teaching biology in the classroom, it is necessary to add a few examples of good models, beginning with the classic series of publications from the Biological Sciences Curriculum Study (BSCS). Very soon after the Soviet Union's success with its Sputnik satellite and the repercussions in America, BSCS was funded by the U.S. National Science Foundation. Its purpose, like those of several other science projects, was to raise the achievement levels of high school students. Early in 1959 work began at a center on the campus of the University of Colorado in Boulder. A steering committee was formed from college biology teachers, education specialists, and high school biology teachers. Over the following 18 months, materials for the classroom were designed, then tested out in classes in 100 schools across the country. Revisions were made to the materials as a result of these tests. The improved materials were then checked out in a different group of schools, 500 in all, involving over a thousand biology teachers, throughout the academic year 1961–62. Alongside all of this activity summer workshops were conducted for other biology teachers, to upgrade their subject knowledge and introduce them to BSCS.

Biological Sciences Curriculum Study

Three main textbooks were published in 1963, each concentrating on a particular aspect of biology, and all of them incorporating the findings of the work of the previous three years. They were known as the blue, green, and yellow books. Before the end of 1963 almost every school district in the nation was using one or more of these texts in its high schools. Predictably, as these books came into widespread use, there was a flurry of activity among creationists because Darwin's theory of evolution was a central theme in all of the BSCS texts. Creationists published book after book at a rate that the country had not seen for decades, to counter the dominance of evolutionary content in the schools. In anticipation of criticism, the new texts noted that evolution might be a new subject for some students. They might even ask if biologists really believe in evolution? The texts went on to say that "believe" is hardly the word to use with respect to a fact of science. Evolution is not a faith but a scientific theory, a theory that has been tested for more than a century against an increasing volume of facts, all of which revised and strengthen it. Darwin knew little about the mechanisms of evolution, but today his basic theory is stronger than ever.

BSCS had to tackle some new things as they developed their texts. For some time schools had tried to cope with the growing volume of new facts that kept appearing by adding content to the school courses, and this was causing a great deal of dissatisfaction. Both students and teachers felt that all they were accomplishing was memorizing quantities of unrelated things. Experts in biology pointed out that the total amount of information about biology, even at that time in 1960, was four times the amount in 1930, and they added that this would continue to increase at an even faster rate. Obviously, they said, we have to be selective about what to include in, and what to leave out of, the school's biological curriculum. Key concepts, ideas that have broad application, must be selected in order to represent adequately the field of biology as a whole. Some leaders of that time, such as Jerome Bruner of Harvard University, suggested that academic subjects should be examined to find what was called their structures. By that was meant ideas that could help explain large amounts of facts, each idea being usable at different levels of the school system. Chapter One describes how an idea of this kind worked for biology when it referred to Dewey's method of teaching science.

This leads to the other major innovation that the BSCS experts had to tackle, how to ensure good scientific method in the classroom, to move the emphases in the schools from authoritative facts to the investigative processes of science. They saw that the accumulation of more and more biological content in the curriculum was creating less and less opportunity for teaching good science. Furthermore, it made it difficult for schools to say that creationism had nothing to do with science if all that was happening in the classroom was memorizing bits of unrelated information. Creationists have never understood that science is not about collecting information only. If they would read Darwin's final words in *The Origin of Species*, they would know that he fully respected the relevance of belief where it belonged, and where science does not belong, as in explanations for the origin of life: "There is grandeur in this view of life, with its several powers, having been originally breathed by the Creator into a few forms or into one; and that, whilst this planet has gone cycling on according to the fixed law of gravity, from so simple a beginning endless forms most beautiful and most wonderful have been, and are being evolved."

To move teachers toward good science, the BSCS leaders defined science as detective work, always involved in problem solving. Educators know nowadays that this is not only good science, it is also the way brains work best. Problems arise out of natural curiosity and both scientists and detectives seek to solve them by formulating hypotheses, then testing each hypothesis against the facts, just as John Dewey did in America for most of the twentieth century. If a particular hypothesis cannot be supported with facts, then a new hypothesis needs to be advanced. It is only when more and more data continue to support a hypothesis that we change it from a hypothesis to a theory. Sometimes it takes a long time to find a solution to a problem as happened with Darwin on one occasion. In 1831, while traveling in the south Pacific, he became very interested in what he called the lagoon islands (atolls). These rings of islands surround a fairly shallow lagoon, a common sight in the warmer areas of the Pacific. On the outer side of the islands the depth of water is very great, quite different from the inside. Darwin wanted to know why atolls are ring-shaped and why they have such a shallow lagoon?

The following hypotheses were suggested by him and by others:

one, they are the craters of extinct volcanoes that now lie deep below the surface and two, coral ridges on the edges of the crater built up to the surface of the ocean. Some years later there was a third hypothesis, that coral ridges were built up around volcanoes during the last ice age when the ocean level dropped to 300 feet below today's level. Depth measurements on the open ocean side of the islands were made by the sailors on Darwin's ship. They found coral, the hard calcium carbonate secreted by certain marine polyps, as far down as 60 feet, then a mixture of coral and sand for the next 120 feet. After that depth there was no more evidence of coral so everyone concluded that the islands must have been built up by coral deposits from some location above the ocean floor. This meant that the first hypothesis was rejected but clearly the second one was still possible and so might the one about the ice age. Darwin suggested that a volcanic mountain might have emerged from the surface of the ocean, coral animals attached themselves to its edges, and still later the volcanic mountain gradually sank.

A subsequent boring on one of the atolls in the Marshall Islands group showed coral rock as far down as 4000 feet below the ocean surface and on the edge of volcanic rock, but we know that coral animals cannot live at depths greater than 350 feet. Darwin's hypothesis and perhaps the ice age one were still viable after this discovery but questions remained as to the origin of such massive volcanoes and their abilities to sink so deeply below the surface of the ocean. The final vindication of Darwin's hypothesis had to wait more than 140 years, until worldwide research on the ocean floor unlocked the secrets of the great tectonic plates. One of the largest of these plates, the Pacific, was found to be moving steadily westward and sometimes northwestward across the Pacific Ocean. As it passed over weak places in the ocean floor, known as hot spots, huge volcanoes erupted and stayed active for millions of years. As they cooled they became heavy and sank. Sometimes the weight was so great that it brought them down to the ocean floor and beyond. The islands that form the State of Hawaii were formed in this way. Thus, in an extreme case like this, the two remaining hypotheses had to wait 140 years to be validated, that is to say proved to be a theory. This is one example of true science.

California

BSCS provided the way forward for all U.S. schools to renew their programs in biological science to the degree that changes were needed. Some states now demonstrate exemplary programs for their high school students, others attempt to do so in the face of strong opposition from creationist groups. Examples of both kinds are included here, beginning with California. Here is a summary of the state's board of education policy on the teaching of natural sciences as of late 2003 together with examples of how the policy plays out in the different grades. While citizens do not have to accept everything that is taught in the natural science curriculum, they do need to understand the major strands of scientific thought, including its methods, facts, hypotheses, and laws. A scientific fact is an understanding based on confirmable observations and is subject to test and rejection. A scientific hypothesis is an attempt to frame a question as a testable proposition. A scientific theory is a logical construct based on facts and hypotheses that organize and explain a range of natural phenomena. Scientific theories are constantly subject to testing, modification, and refutation as new evidence emerges and, because they have predictive capabilities, they guide further investigations.

These statements are valuable guidelines, all completely in keeping with the goals expressed in the BSCS books, and they help to maintain the distinctiveness of science in the public mind as well as with school administrators. They have particular relevance to the type of concluding statement that likely refers to creationists and which the board felt it had to make. From time to time teachers of natural science are asked to teach content that does not meet the criteria of scientific fact, hypothesis, or theory. Science teachers are professionally bound to limit their teaching to science and resist pressures to do otherwise. The administrators of schools should always support teachers in relation to this. In California, the study of evolution begins in grade two with foundational notions of inheritance, variation within species, and an introduction to fossils. Grade three deals with adaptation to an environment and the processes of extinction. In grade four students learn about the survivability of

165

plants and animals within their environments. Grade seven introduces the idea of natural selection and a more detailed examination of the fossil record as the main line of evidence for evolution. Finally, at the high school level, there are in-depth studies of biology.

Michigan

As of the beginning of 2004, the state of Michigan was under severe pressure from creationists to accept changes to its science programs. The views of specialists within the state board of education and the Michigan Science Teachers Association were diametrically opposed to those of at least 34 members of the House of Representatives. It is not often that one finds among U.S. states so many elected members opposed to the views of the specialists they had previously chosen to advise them on educational matters. Choice of subject content at the high school level is not a matter of democratic choice any more than the dates of historical events are matters of opinion. No member of a legislature should be expected to act as a specialist in science, yet that is what these 34 members have proposed. Here are a few of the details of the creationists' bills in order to compare them with BSCS statements, now the norm for the teaching of biological science anywhere in the country. The Michigan Science Teachers Position Statement on the teaching of evolution follow, and it forms a valuable endorsement of BSCS.

Bill 4946 proposed, among other things, (a) that all references to evolution be modified to indicate that it is an unproven theory and (b) that the theory that life is the result of the intelligent design of a creator be taught. BSCS made it clear that the first part of the statement is false and the second has nothing to do with science since it is not open to validation or rejection experimentally. Bill 5005 stated that the teaching of the methodological naturalism hypothesis as an explanation for the origin of life shall not preclude also teaching the design hypothesis as an explanation for the origin of life. Both parts of this statement are irrelevant to science. Scientists deal with life once it exists, not before. U.S. Supreme Court decisions have pointed this out more than once. It is difficult to understand why legislators would want to introduce such anarchic notions and try to impose them on schools against the views of experts and in violation of U.S. Supreme Court decisions. Perhaps the desire to curry favor with voters overrides all other considerations. By contrast the following position statement of the Michigan Science Teachers Association (MSTA) is a model of proper behavior, an example to both legislators and their fellow teachers across the country:

> We adopt the position statement of the National Science Teachers Association (NSTA) as outlined in their web site www.nsta.org regarding the teaching of evolution. Darwin's basic theory of evolution is a major unifying concept of science and should be part of biological science curricula at all levels of the school system. MSTA recognizes that evolution has not been emphasized in science curricula in a manner commensurate with its importance because of official policies, intimidation of science teachers, the general public's misunderstanding of evolutionary theory, and a century of controversy. Furthermore, teachers are being pressured to introduce creationism, creation science, and other nonscientific views which are intended to weaken or eliminate the teaching of evolution. In recognition of the Michigan State Board of Education's resolution on the teaching of evolution, MSTA advocates that bills 4946 and 5005 be removed from any further consideration by the House of Representatives.

North Carolina

North Carolina's precision of language in its descriptions of biological science programs is impressive. The obfuscation that is found in the programs of some states is completely absent here. At the end of grade twelve, all students should have constructed an understanding of the following concepts, theories, and universal laws: the cell, molecular basis of heredity, biological evolution, interdependence of organisms, energy in the earth systems, geochemical cycles, origin and evolution of the earth system, and origin and evolution of the universe. These summaries are followed by useful statements about scientific method, the aspect of school work that was of greatest concern to the BSCS people. Here are some of the North Carolina statements included in the curriculum guides:

> In science, explanations are limited to those that can be inferred from confirmable data. When observations of a phenomenon are confirmed or can be repeated, they are regarded as fact. Any scientific confirmation is, however, tentative, because it is always possible that the results occurred by chance.
>
> A scientific theory is a body of continually refined observation, inference, and testable hypotheses. Because science is never irrevocably committed to any theory, no matter how firmly it appears to be established, it can never be dogmatic. Any theory is always subject to change in the light of new and confirmed observations. Students should be taught that uncertainty is not a weakness, but a strength that leads to self-correction. Theories explain phenomena that we observe. They are never proved. Rather they represent the most logical explanation to date for the phenomena. Theories become stronger as more supporting evidence is gathered. They also provide a context for further research and help us make predictions. The theory of biological evolution is a well documented explanation for the diversity of species. Gene theory is an explanation for the relationships we observe between generations. Laws in science are quite different from theories. They are universal generalizations based on observations of the natural world. The nature of gravity, the nature of planetary movement, and the relationships of forces and motions are all examples of laws.

Ohio

Few states took the same trouble as Ohio to find out public opinion before finalizing its present science curricula. Over 18,000 responses were received from the public over the course of the year 2002 in reply to a request that people identify their wishes within three categories: creationism only, creationism and evolution, and evolution only. The state authorities had been under a great deal of pressure from creationists and it decided to measure the level and form of that pressure. They had good reason to be concerned. Of the 18,000 responses, most of them wanted both evolution and creationism taught in the science classroom. This is the most common form of creationist overtures across the U.S. and clearly Ohio was singled out for special attention, probably because public opinion was sympathetic to the idea of including creationism. From the point of view of the reforms that BSCS initiated, any move of this kind would be the death knell of good science. Fortunately, Ohio chose to reject any inclusion of creationism.

The benchmarks, the data that will be examined in Ohio's assessments, that are identified at the grade ten level of science are clear indications of the failure of creationist pressures: Benchmark One, explain the 4.5 billion-year-history of life on earth based on observable scientific evidence in the geologic record; Benchmark Two, Explain the historical and current scientific developments, mechanisms, and processes of biological evolution; Benchmark Three, Describe how scientists continue to investigate and critically analyze aspects of evolutionary theory (this has nothing to do with teaching or testing intelligent design); Benchmark Four, Explain how natural selection and other evolutionary mechanisms account for the unity and diversity of past and present life forms; Benchmark Five, Summarize the historical development of scientific theories and ideas, and describe emerging issues in the study of life sciences.

Pennsylvania

The final model comes from Pennsylvania where detailed goals for four different grade levels are given. All of these deal with biological sciences and they are preceded by the following statement: "Pennsylvania's public schools shall teach, challenge and support every student to realize his or her maximum potential and to acquire the knowledge and skills needed":

Grade 4:
A. Know the similarities and differences of living things. Identify life processes of living things (e.g. growth, digestion, react to environment).
   1. Know that some organisms have similar external characteristics (e.g. anatomical characteristics, appendages,

169

type of covering, body segments) and that similarities and differences are related to environmental habitat.

2. Describe basic needs of plants and animals.

B. Know that living things are made up of parts that have specific functions.

    1. Identify examples of unicellular and multicellular organisms.

    2. Determine how different parts of a living thing work together to make the organism function.

C. Know that characteristics are inherited and, thus, offspring closely resemble their parents.

    1. Identify characteristics for animal and plant survival in different climates.

    2. Identify physical characteristics that appear in both parents and offspring and differ between families, strains or species.

D. Identify changes in living things over time. Compare extinct life forms with living organisms.

Grade 7:

A. Describe the similarities and differences that characterize diverse living things.

    1. Describe how the structures of living things help them function in unique ways.

    2. Explain how to use a dichotomous key to identify plants and animals.

    3. Account for adaptations among organisms that live in a particular environment.

B. Describe the cell as the basic structural and functional unit of living things.

    1. Identify the levels of organization from cell to organism.

    2. Compare life processes at the organism level with life processes at the cell level.

    3. Explain that cells and organisms have particular structures that underlie their functions.

    4. Describe and distinguish among cell cycles, reproductive cycles and life cycles.

    5. Explain disease effects on structures or functions of an organism.

C. Know that every organism has a set of genetic instructions that determines its inherited traits.

   1. Identify and explain inheritable characteristics.
   2. Identify that the gene is the basic unit of inheritance.
   3. Identify basic patterns of inheritance (e.g., dominance, recessive, co-dominance).
   4. Describe how traits are inherited.
   5. Distinguish how different living things reproduce (e.g., vegetative budding, sexual).
   6. Recognize that mutations can alter a gene.
   7. Describe how selective breeding, natural selection and genetic technologies can change genetic makeup of organisms.
D. Explain basic concepts of natural selection.
   1. Identify adaptations that allow organisms to survive in their environment.
   2. Describe how an environmental change can affect the survival of organisms and entire species.
   3. Know that differences in individuals of the same species may give some advantage in surviving and reproducing.
   4. Recognize that populations of organisms can increase rapidly.
   5. Describe the role that fossils play in studying the past.
   6. Explain how biologic extinction is a natural process.

Grade 10:
A. Explain the structural and functional similarities and differences found among living things.
   1. Identify and characterize major life forms according to their placement in existing classification groups.
   2. Explain the relationship between structure and function at the molecular and cellular levels.
   3. Describing organizing schemes of classification keys.
   4. Identify and characterize major life forms by kingdom, phyla, class and order.
B. Describe and explain the chemical and structural basis of living organisms.
   1. Describe the relationship between the structure of organic molecules and the function they serve in living organisms.
   2. Identify the specialized structures and regions of the cell and the functions of each.
   3. Explain how cells store and use information to guide their functions.

4. Explain cell functions and processes in terms of chemical reactions and energy changes.

C. Describe how genetic information is inherited and expressed.
1. Compare and contrast the function of mitosis and meiosis.
2. Describe mutations' effects on a trait's expression.
3. Distinguish different reproductive patterns in living things (e.g., budding, spores, fission).
4. Compare random and selective breeding practices and their results (e.g., antibiotic resistant bacteria).
5. Explain the relationship among DNA, genes and chromosomes.
6. Explain different types of inheritance (e.g., multiple allele, sex-influenced traits).
7. Describe the role of DNA in protein synthesis as it relates to gene expression.

D. Explain the mechanisms of the theory of evolution.
1. Analyze data from fossil records, similarities in anatomy and physiology, embryological studies and DNA studies that are relevant to the theory of evolution.
2. Explain the role of mutations and gene recombination in changing a population of organisms.
3. Compare modern day descendants of extinct species and propose possible scientific accounts for their present appearance.
4. Describe the factors (e.g., isolation, differential reproduction) affecting gene frequency in a population over time and their consequences.
5. Describe and differentiate between the roles of natural selection and genetic drift.
6. Describe the changes that illustrate major events in the earth's development based on a time line.
7. Explain why natural selection can act only on inherited traits.
8. Apply the concept of natural selection to illustrate and account for a species' survival, extinction or change over time.

Grade 12:
A. Explain the relationship between structure and function at all levels of organization.

    1. Identify and explain interactions among organisms (e.g., mutually beneficial, harmful relationships).

    2. Explain and analyze the relationship between structure and function at the molecular, cellular and organ-system level.

    3. Describe and explain structural and functional relationships in each of the five (or six) kingdoms.

    4. Explain significant biological diversity found in each of the biomes.

B. Analyze the chemical and structural basis of living organisms.

    1. Identify and describe factors affecting metabolic function (e.g., temperature, acidity, hormones).

    2. Evaluate metabolic activities using experimental knowledge of enzymes.

    3. Evaluate relationships between structure and functions of different anatomical parts given their structure.

    4. Describe potential impact of genome research on the biochemistry and physiology of life.

C. Explain gene inheritance and expression at the molecular level.

    1. Analyze gene expression at the molecular level.

    2. Describe the roles of nucleic acids in cellular reproduction and protein synthesis.

    3. Describe genetic engineering techniques, applications and impacts.

    4. Explain birth defects from the standpoint of embryological development and/or changes in genetic makeup.

D. Analyze the theory of evolution.

    1. Examine human history by describing the progression from early hominids to modern humans.

    2. Apply the concept of natural selection as a central concept in illustrating evolution theory.

Through programs like Pennsylvania's, good biology teaching can be recovered for the schools. If one looks again at this state's academic standards for grade ten students certain features stand out. Students are asked to classify life forms in different ways, to identify structural and functional relationships at the cell level, to analyze data from fossils, and to explain genetic engineering methods.

There are no lists of names and distinguishing characteristics of hundreds of plants and animals, yet, despite the futility of this old style of teaching, it is still a common pattern of instruction in schools. The recovery that is needed is method, not facts, the kind of change that was and is being advocated by the BSCS designers.

To them the accumulation of facts about science hinders rather than helps good science. In their textbooks they often incorporated statements of uncertainty and incompleteness in order to emphasize that science is always a process of inquiry, seeking to reduce uncertainty and make knowledge more complete but never arriving at a final answer. It is a method of advancing through investigations, experiments, data, and interpretation of data, but never reaching a place where everything is known. Creationists mistakenly assume that science consists of a closed body of facts, so they counter with their own alternative set of facts. The best answer to their misguided outlook is a display of the scientific method.

Appendix

Five Common Questions About Evolution

Q: I thought that evolution was a theory. Why is it called a fact?

A: Biological evolution is a change of organisms from an original simple one to the present day life forms. That is fact. There is no universal agreement on the mechanisms by which these changes occur.

Q: No one has observed evolution happening so how do you know that it is true?

A: Evolution has been observed in both labs and in fossils.

Q: Why has no one seen a new species appear?

A: New species have been observed in both labs and in nature.

Q: If evolution is the result of chance does that not make it an improbable event?

A: Evolution is the result of both random and non-random events.

Q: How do you know that the earth is very old?

A: Various independent dating methods are used.

Glossary

Adaptation: Features of organisms that aid survival and reproduction.

Allele: A gene that occupies a particular place on a chromosome.

Amino acid: The basic building block of a protein. In the average living organism, there are as many as 20 of these amino acids.

Bacteria: Microorganisms that show an enormous range of abilitiescapable of living in extremes of temperature and other difficult environmental conditions.

Biological determinism: The claim that the characteristics of organisms are due to their genes only and therefore not subject to environment.

Burgess Shale: A sedimentary unit that is part of a formation in the Rocky Mountains of British Columbia. This formation is over 500 million years old and is known worldwide for its enormous quantity of fossils.

Catastrophism: A belief that earth's history is dominated by major upheavals.

Chromosome: Threadlike links that carry the genes within the center of a cell.

Cladistics: The science of identifying characteristics that determine whether species are distantly or closely related.

Cladogram: A diagram showing species that are closely related historically, that is descended from the same source.

Contingency: A more technical term for the word chance and is the notion that unexpected events occur.

Craton: The nucleus of a continent, very often 10 or 15 miles thick, consisting mainly of granitic rocks. A craton is very stable with little earthquake and volcanic action.

Glossary

Creation science: A system claiming that scientific evidence supports the story of creation in the early part of the book of Genesis.

Darwinism: A term usually applied to Darwin's statement that natural selection is the main causal factor in evolution.

Day-age creationism: A view that relates to scientific findings by interpreting each of the six days of creation as very long periods of time.

Deism: A belief that God works only through fixed laws without using miracles.

Disparity: The variety of different types of animal fossils found at any one period of time, each type of animal having the same basic anatomy and morphology.

Diversity: The total number of species or higher levels of organisms at a given point of time.

DNA: The molecule that transmits genetic information.

Empiricism: The view that knowledge must be based on experience through the five senses.

Evolutionary creationism: The view that God, as creator, uses the method of evolution to form the universe.

Flat earthers: People who believe that the shape of the earth is flat, based on a literal reading of the Bible.

Gap creationists: People who say there is a huge time gap between Genesis 1:1 and Genesis 1: 2 and that this gap explains the apparent great age of the earth.

Genetic drift: Accidents of mating in small populations that can outweigh the effects of natural selection.

Genome: The totality of DNA in an organism.

Genotype: An organism's genetic information as distinct from its phenotype.

Geocentrists: Those who deny that the sun is the center of the solar system. This was the commonly-held view 4,000 years ago.

Geological time: Time measured by radiometric methods, that is to say the measurement of the decay of radioactive substances which is a constant and tells how old a particular rock is.

Hominids: Forms of life anatomically similar to humans, able to walk on two legs.

Intelligent design creationists: A modern form of natural theology, the view that the work of a creator is evident in creation.

Metazoans: Another word for animals that refers to the total group that is represented by that word, sometimes referred to as one of the six kingdoms of life, the largest category of living things.

Molluscs: Sea creatures with broad feet for getting around and protected by a shell.

Morphology: The study of organic form.

Natural selection: Darwin's explanation for evolutionary change, namely that a small percentage of organisms in each generation survive and reproduce because they possess characteristics which other members of the same group do not possess.

Natural theology: The long standing view that something of the nature of the creator can be seen in his creation.

Neanderthals: An extinct hominid sub-species that shares common features with modern humans.

Old-earth creationists: People who accept the great age of the earth but insist that God was and is personally involved as an active agent.

Paleontologist: A person who studies fossils.

Pelagic: Organisms that either swim or float in water.

Phenotype: The visible and behavior characteristics of an organism.

Phylogeny: The term used to define the study of evolution, particularly the relationships between organisms and the various ways that they branch through time.

Phylum: A technical term describing a major grouping of organisms. It's a scheme that ranks next below a kingdom.

Plankton: Organisms that float in the water column.

Plate tectonics: Term for the layer of surface rock that lies at the bottom of the sea and is constantly moving under pressure from volcanic action below.

Progressive creationism: A view that evolution occurred among groups at a higher level than species but a rejection that all forms of life have a common ancestry.

Speciation: The formation of new species.

Species: The basic unit of biology, defined on the basis of the group's ability to interbreed and produce fertile offspring.

Taxonomic hierarchy: The different categories of biology between the phylum and the species. They usually amount to in ascending order from the species: genus, family, order, and class.

Glossary

Theism: The belief that God intervenes in his creation.

Trace fossil: The remains of the activity of an organism, including a hole or a burrow left by a worm or a trail left by a sea creature.

Trilobites: An extinct animal that flourished prior to 250 million years ago.

Uniformitarianism: The claim that events in the geological past can be explained in terms of those operating today.

Vertebrates: A large group of organisms which includes mammals, birds, reptiles, fish and amphibians.

Young-earth creationists: Those who reject modern views of the age of the earth and insist that it is only thousands rather than billions of years old.

Bibliography

Aldridge, Bill G. (Ed.). *Scope, Sequence, and Coordination: A High School Framework for Science Education*. Arlington, VA: National Science Teachers Association (NSTA), 1996.

Alexander, Denis. *Rebuilding the Matrix: Science and Faith in the 21st Century*. Grand Rapids, MI: Zondervan, 2003.

American Association for the Advancement of Science (AAAS), Project 2061. *Benchmarks for Science Literacy*. New York: Oxford University Press, 1993.

Asimov, Isaac. *In the Beginning*. New York: Crown Publishers, 1981.

Bebbington, David. *Evangelicalism in Modern Britain: A History from the 1730s to the 1980s*. London: Unwin Hyman/Routledge, 1989.

Behe, Michael J. *Darwin's Black Box: The Biochemical Challenge to Evolution*. New York: Free Press, 1996.

Boorstin, Daniel J. *The Discoverers: A History of Man's Search to Know His World and Himself*. New York: Random House, 1985.

Crane, Nicholas. *Mercator: The Man Who Mapped the Planet*. London: Weidenfeld and Nicholson, 2002.

Cuvier, Georges. *Essay on the Theory of the Earth*. Edinburgh: William Blackwood, 1817.

Danielson, Dennis R. *The Book of the Cosmos: Imagining the Universe from Heraclitus to Hawking*. Cambridge, MA: Perseus Publishing, 2000.

Darwin, Charles R. *On the Origin of Species by Means of Natural Selection*. London: John Murray, 1859.

Dawkins, Richard. *The Selfish Gene*. New York: Oxford University Press, 1976.

De Hamel, Christopher. *The Book: A History of the Bible*. London: Phaidon Press Limited, 2001.

Dembski, William A., and Kushiner, James M. *Signs of Intelligence*. Grand Rapids, MI: Brazos Press, 2001.

Department of Divinity, University of Aberdeen. *But Where Shall Wisdom Be Found?* Initium Sapientiae Timor Domini. Aberdeen: Aberdeen University Press, 1995.

Bibliography

Devine, T. M. *The Scottish Nation: 1700–2000.* London: Penguin Group, 1999.

Eldridge, Niles. *The Triumph of Evolution and the Failure of Creationism.* New York: William Freeman, 2000.

Eve, Raymond A., and Harrold, Francis B. *The Creationist Movement in Modern America.* Boston: Twayne, 1991.

Gould, Stephen Jay. *Rocks of Ages: Science and Religion in the Fullness of Life.* New York: Random House, 1999.

_____. *The Structure of Evolutionary Theory.* Cambridge, MA: Harvard University Press, 2002.

Huggett, Richard. *Cataclysms and Earth History.* New York: Oxford University Press, 1989.

Hutton, James. *Theory of the Earth with Proofs and Illustrations,* 2 Vols. Edinburgh: William Creech, 1795.

Johnson, Paul. *Modern Times: The World from the Twenties to the Eighties.* New York: Harper and Row, 1983.

Johnson, Phillip E. *Reason in the Balance: The Case Against Naturalism in Science.* Downers Grove, IL: InterVarsity Press, 1995.

La Follette, Marclel C. (Ed). *Creationism, Science, and the Law: The Arkansas Case.* Cambridge, MA: MIT Press..

Larson, Edward J. *Trial and Error: The American Controversy Over Creation and Evolution.* 3rd ed. New York: Oxford University Press, 2003.

Lerner, Lawrence S. *Good Science, Bad Science: Teaching Evolution in the States.* Washington, DC: Thomas B. Fordham Foundation, 2000.

Malthus, Thomas. *An Essay on the Principle of Population as It Affects the Future Improvement of Society.* London: J. Johnson, 1798.

Morris, Henry M. *The Genesis Flood: The Biblical Record and Its Scientific Implications.* Philadelphia: Presbyterian and Reformed Publishing Company, 1961.

_____, and Parker, Gary E. *What Is Creation Science?* El Cajon, CA: Creation-Life Publishers, 1982.

Morris, Richard. *The Evolutionists: The Struggle for Darwin's Soul.* New York: Henry Holt, 2001.

Morris, S. Conway. *The Crucible of Creation: The Burgess Shale and the Rise of Animals.* New York: Oxford University Press, 1998.

Moynahan, Brian. *If God Spare My Life: William Tyndale, the English Bible and Sir Thomas More; A Story of Martyrdom and Betrayal.* London: Little, Brown, 2002.

National Research Council. *The National Science Education Standards.* Washington, DC: National Academy Press, 1996.

New Revised Standard Version Bible. New York: Division of Christian Education of the National Council of Churches of Christ in the U.S.A., 1989.

Numbers, Ronald L. *The Creationists*. New York: Alfred A. Knopf, 1992.
_____. *Darwin Comes to America*. Cambridge, MA: Harvard University Press, 1998.
Pickering, James S. *Asterisks: A Book of Astronomical Footnotes*. New York: Dodd, Mead, 1964.
Polanyi, Michael. *Personal Knowledge*. London: Routledge and Kegan Paul, 1958.
Polkinghorne, John. *Belief in God in an Age of Science*. New Haven: Yale University Press, 1998.
Ruse, Michael. *Darwin and Design*. Cambridge, MA: Harvard University Press, 2003.
Ryan, William, and Pitman, Walter. *Noah's Flood: The New Scientific Discoveries About the Event That Changed History*. New York: Simon and Schuster, 1998.
Santillana, Georgio de. *The Crime of Galileo*. Chicago: University of Chicago Press, 1955.
Singer, Charles. *A Short History of Scientific Ideas to 1900*. Oxford: The Clarendon Press, 1959.
Stewart, John. *Evolution's Arrow: The Direction of Evolution and the Future of Humanity*. Canberra, Australia: Chapman Press, 2000.
Young, Willard. *Fallacies of Creationism*. Calgary: Detselik Enterprises Ltd, 1985

Index

Index

DATE DUE

GAYLORD   PRINTED IN U.S.A.